Praise for *A Group I Never Wanted to Join*

"*A Group I Never Wanted to Join* is filled with real-life stories that ooze hope for recovery from grief. Tender, sincere, honest, encouraging. Marty McNunn has captured the difficulty and delicateness of living through grief in a manner that gives the reader permission to accept and express the emotions of loss. Marty McNunn applies time-tested wisdom and experience to a life situation we can all relate to. Her depth of knowledge and breadth of relationships as well as her understanding of loss and the means to rise above it shine through. This book will educate and assist anyone who is walking through the maze of emotions, questions and challenges that grief engenders."

Pastor Jeff Utecht
Evangel United Methodist Church, Rochester, Minnesota

"Marty's wisdom and knowledge, combined with people's unique experiences make reading this book a delight. It is a wonderful compilation . . . Simple, yet profound, intensely personal, yet universal. All will benefit from reading this book."

Lisa Graham, MA, LSW, medical social worker

"This book outlines a wide spectrum of the various aspects of the grieving process. It will be helpful and inspiring, especially to those who lose a loved one by death, . . . and also a resource to those who sustain other major losses."

Lew Linde
Lawyer, social worker, and author of Lew and Marcella

"Those grieving the loss of a loved one will benefit greatly by the many personal and inspiring grief journeys shared in this book to give hope and encouragement to others beginning a similar journey."

Marge Eaton Heegaard, director
Coalitions for Grief Support, Minneapolis-Saint Paul area

For Barb,
my High
School friend.

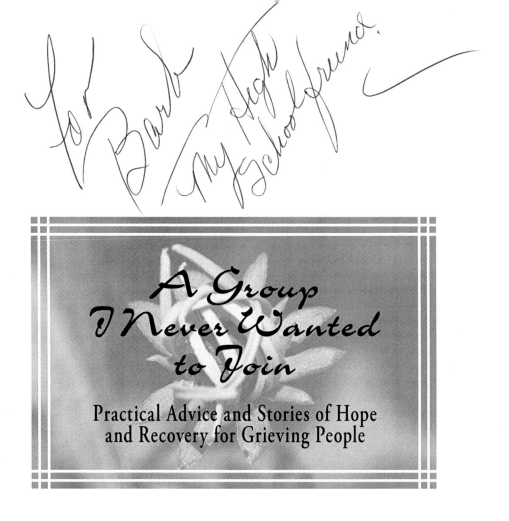

A Group I Never Wanted to Join

Practical Advice and Stories of Hope and Recovery for Grieving People

MARTY McNUNN

Marty McNunn
3 John 2

SYREN BOOK COMPANY
MINNEAPOLIS

Most Syren Books are available at special quantity discounts for bulk purchases for sales promotions, premiums, fund-raising, and educational needs. For details, write

Syren Book Company
Special Sales Department
5120 Cedar Lake Road
Minneapolis, MN 55416

Published by
Syren Book Company
5120 Cedar Lake Road
Minneapolis, MN 55416

Printed in the United States of America on acid-free paper

ISBN-13: 978-0-929636-67-2
ISBN-10: 0-929636-67-8

LCCN 2006926238

Cover design by Kyle G. Hunter
Cover photo from the collection of Vivian Walker
in memory of Elora Grace Howard
Book design by Ann Sudmeier

To order additional copies of this book see the form
at the back of this book or go to www.itascabooks.com

This book is written for people grieving
a loved one's death.
It is written to help them see at a glance
how grief feels and how it affects them.
It is also intended to help others understand
what it means to grieve, since
no one really understands grief until he or she
has experienced the loss of a significant person.

My very special thanks to all of you grieving
people who participate
in the Hastings Area Grief Coalition.

Your feelings, confusion, and hurts,
your laughter, your stories,
your sharing of thoughts,
and your commitment to
finding wholeness
make this book
possible.

*Life goes on;
you will find peace.
May God bless your days.*

Contents

—

What Is Grief?

—

Suffering the loss of a loved one
Extreme anguish: emotional, physical, psychological, and spiritual
An experience caused by the loss of a loved one
A process of adapting to change you did not ask for

A forced journey that you must travel alone
A roller coaster ride of emotions
A wave that engulfs you
A changing sea of emotions

A unique and personal experience
Life without joy
A great empty space
A knife that keeps turning in the chest

An extreme heartache
A black hole, a pit with no light
A lonely trip
An unfair experience

An experience no one can escape
Like trying to put a square peg in a round hole

When the sun is shaded by a cloud,

the moon has no luster,

and the stars no longer shine.

Mourning
Expressing grief and great sorrow,
inner anguish, weeping, audible sounds or sobs.
It is the process of working through grief.

Common Feelings

———

Sorrow, sadness, disorientation
Sleepiness, fear, bitterness
Achiness, rage, blurry vision
Lethargy, feeling scared or lost

Anger, guilt, suicidal tendencies, sick
Panic, uselessness, despair
Emptiness, heartbreak, desperation
Confused, in shock, separated, hostile

Exhausted, restless, robot-like
Hopeless, self-pitying, frustrated
Clammy, fatigued, cold or hot
Disbelief, lack of motivation

Anger at God, loss of faith
Depressed, insane, insecure
Vague, inept, like a zombie

In short: Nothing feels right.

Common Physical Symptoms

Stomach problems
Heart palpitations
Fatigue, headaches
Dry mouth/thirst

Blurred vision, tingling
Shortness of breath
Heaviness, backaches
Weight gain or loss

Numbness
Unexplained pain,
all over, anytime, for no reason

Common Thoughts

This can't be happening to me.
What will become of me?
What have I done wrong?
I am so scared.
I'll never get over this.

I can't handle this.
It's too much for me.
I wish I were dead.
Why couldn't it have been me?
I should have done more.
Who's going to hug me now?

I can't do this alone.
What do I do now?
I am so confused.
Why me, why me, why me?
Will I ever recover?
Where is God in all of this?

I Think I'm Going Crazy

I can't remember:
what day it is; to eat and drink; to feed the dog
where I parked the car; my own kids' names; to pay the bills
to buy groceries or to take my medications

where I am; where I live; where I'm going
what I'm supposed to do; to keep appointments
to look at my calendar; to water my flowers
to comb my hair or brush my teeth
to take a shower.

I lose my keys, my car, my shoes,
my friend, my job;
I'm so confused, so lost, so hopeless:
I have no interest in life.

I've lost my faith. I can't find God and I'm not sure I want to;
I cry and cry and cry, and then I cry some more: I fear I can't stop.

Dear Reader:
No, you are not going crazy. You're grieving!

Ten Common Misstatements

Many well-intentioned people have misconceptions about the grief process. In a genuine, but misguided, effort to be helpful, they may make misstatements such as those that follow. Dear grieving person, please remember that you do not always need to listen to free advice!

Misstatement 1: It's been six months (a year, two years)—you should be over it by now.

Grief has no time limit. It is individual and has no expiration date. Working towards recovery takes a long time. More than that, you never "get over losing a loved one." You learn to live with the loss. Life goes on and you *will* begin to feel alive again.

Misstatement 2: It's time you quit crying.

Sorry, no expiration date on crying, either. Crying is a natural part of loss. In the beginning you cry often for no reason, or when prompted by a thought, a memory, a smell, or a special day. Tears are God-given for the healing of your broken heart. Crying does occur less and less often. Still, even years later, talking about your loved one can bring a tear or two. Scripture tell us that God holds our tears in a bottle. He believes they are special.

Misstatement 3: Life will be normal again soon.

Losing a significant person to death changes your life. Everything that was normal will never seem normal again. Activities that included your loved one will never be the same because that special person is missing. What can you do now? It's important to begin to create for yourself a "new normal" life. Small changes in your daily activities, holidays, and family celebrations are all helpful steps you can initiate.

Misstatement 4: Go back to work or get a job.

Going back to work or getting a new job will not do anything for your grief. It will simply fill your hours with busyness. Often that busyness can delay the grief process because it leaves you no time to take care of your emotions or to allow yourself to grieve. Grieving doesn't work on an 8-to-5 schedule. In fact, busyness may block your responses, causing you to pretend everything is okay, when in reality you are only suppressing your feelings.

Misstatement 5: Time heals.

Yes and no. It isn't the time that heals—it's what you do during that time. Time does help you adjust to your loss, but it only helps, it doesn't heal. Healing from grief is nothing like healing from surgery or illness, where we expect everything to be all right in six or eight weeks. It's very common for grieving people to feel as if they will never recover, but as they work towards healing, life begins to adjust to their loss. Soon life will be moving in a positive direction, and they will find joy again. Time does help the process. On the other hand, a crushed heart seldom heals completely. Instead, it learns to cope with the scars.

Misstatement 6: You talk about him or her too much.

As a grieving person, you need to talk about your loved one. It's part of the healing process. You have a story to tell, so tell your story often. Your loved one's presence is still with you. Although he or she may be dead, your loved one's spirit is still here in your heart and in the nearness of your love—just in another realm. Talking about your loved one is good for the healing process.

Misstatement 7: I know how you feel.

Not really. Even if someone has lost a loved one to the same type of death, each person's grief is personal and different. Your relationship and the circumstances with your loved one will not be exactly the same as those of any other person. It's not necessary to identify with the death to bring comfort and support. A listening ear and a gentle hug work wonders.

Misstatement 8: It's God's will. He must have needed him or her in heaven.

I believe this statement is one of the worst a person can make. How does another person know what God's will is for you? Why would God tell someone else His will for you? And God does not need your loved one in heaven. He is perfectly capable of taking care of heaven on His own. God and the grieving person may not be on very good speaking terms at this particular time: no need to make it worse. In Psalm 139, Scripture tells us that "God knows the days of each life."

As I understand it, He does not make a person die on a certain day, but He knows about the death. No one knows why a child has to die, or why a teen is killed, or why someone chooses to take his or her own life. Death is part of life. People die for all kinds of reasons. When we learn to live with our loss (and eventually we do), most often our experience makes us a better person.

The Lord's loved ones are precious to him.
He grieves when they die.
PSALM 116:15 (NLT)

Misstatement 9: There are seven stages of grief.

Since grief is not a normal part of your life, you can't organize your feelings and thoughts in stages. You may experience three, four, five, or more different feelings in a day. If that isn't enough, it seems they all return the next day, bringing even more feelings with them and even changing from what they were a day earlier. Feelings are fickle; they come and go like a yo-yo, and your feelings just won't fit into anyone else's pattern.

Misstatement 10: Just pray and read your Bible.

Praying and reading the Bible is good. However, praying and reading alone will not heal your grief. Yes, praying helps, and yes, seeking comfort in the Scriptures helps. But those activities alone do not heal your grief. It takes time to come back to faith and find comfort once more in a relationship with the Lord. Like many, you may experience anger toward God and blame Him for your grief. That's okay; He understands.

The First Year

—

It's common knowledge that the first year following the death of a loved one is the hardest.

During this time, you:
- are adjusting to the loss of your loved one's presence
- don't feel like celebrating
- are not motivated to make plans
- are not comfortable in crowds
- dread all those special days without him or her, including birthdays, your anniversary, Mother's Day, Father's Day
- find that the holidays everybody celebrates, such as Easter, Thanksgiving and Christmas, aren't the same to you anymore.

As a grieving person, you must make a choice:
- Will you allow your grief to spoil your day, as well as the day of other family and friends?

Remember, the rest of your family needs its celebration traditions, as new memories are made every year.

Will you be overcome by fear that:
- you might cry?
- you might get angry?
- you might be depressed?
- you might be sad all day?

Or, will you move forward towards healing and restoration, and make plans to have a good day?

However, if you purposely choose to have a good day:
- you might enjoy yourself, or laugh a little, or feel a little joy
- you might enjoy visiting with family and friends
- you might receive so many hugs that your sadness disappears
- you might enjoy the taste of good food
- it might turn out to be a really good day

The choice becomes yours.

It's likely that everyone in your family has lost a special person; you are not alone in your grief. Other family members dread these special days, too. Each of you grieves differently. This is not a normal celebration because someone is missing, but as you share this experience you are beginning to make new traditions and create "new normals" for your family's special days.

You may choose to continue with the same traditions, or you may decide to make a new one that is more appropriate to the family as it is now.

Yes, the choice is yours.

You and your family must decide how you want to proceed this year. That doesn't mean you will do the same things next year. You plan one year at a time.

Here are some suggestions to help you get started:
- Rather than the usual celebration, make the day a time for remembering the lost and celebrating the living.
- Decide who will host the family gathering this year.
- Decide how you want to be involved.
- Be honest with your family.
- Say no if you want to; it's okay.
- Simplify the activities for the actual day, at least for this year.
- Be wise about advance preparations; your energy levels are not the same.
- Share the shopping, preparation, arrangements, and cleanup.

Honor your loved one with:
- a special candle to light at all family occasions
- telling stories
- sharing memories
- making a donation to a charity in his or her name
- planting a tree

Be creative: When special days of the year arrive, there are many ways to honor the one you've lost.

How Do I Get Over Grief?

Grieving is a process of adapting to a change you didn't want, a process of acknowledging that life as you knew it will never be the same.

Suggestions that others have found helpful in overcoming grief:
- Acknowledge your loss
- Recognize that life will not be the same ever again
- Accept that what was normal is no longer normal
- Begin to create "new normals"
- Keep your memories alive
- Give yourself time to grieve; don't rush the process
- Be patient
- Educate yourself about the process
- Choose to stay positive
- Cry when you need to
- Have a daily exercise plan
- Get plenty of rest and eat well-balanced meals
- Don't spend your days alone
- Stay in contact with family and friends
- Let others grieve in their own way
- Pray

- Attend worship services
- Join a grief support group
- Seek counsel
- Have faith for your future
- Set short- and long-term goals
- Create a memory book
- Plant a memorial garden
- Don't give up; persevere

You will get through this.

Death of a Spouse

Char's Story

CHAR VICK

My husband, Jim, and I led an extremely hectic and interesting life. We'd lived in Minnesota, Wisconsin, and Alaska. We have five children, four of whom were adopted, had some disabilities, and were of different races. Jim was a teacher also holding local political offices. Once a lawyer who specialized in poverty law, I now work in the area of adoptions. Because our middle daughter has addiction problems, we also took on the challenge of raising our granddaughter. We have five grandchildren.

Then Jim died suddenly of a heart attack at the age of sixty. I couldn't believe that my beautiful, loving partner, lover, best friend, mate, and co-workhorse was gone. We were a couple of kids who came from tough homes and found each other. We had built an amazingly good marriage and accomplished many things in our lives. I used to tell him that, if he ever left, I would curl up into a ball and stay in bed. I haven't—but I could have. The death of someone so close is absolutely the worst thing that can happen to a person. Even now, two and a half years later, I can't write about it without crying.

The experts talk about shock. I think that's what kept me going for the first few months. Also, I had my ten-year-old granddaughter and my Alzheimer's-challenged mother-in-law to care for.

Early in my grief I decided to attend a local grief group. Of all my efforts to find some solace, this was the most effective. The facilitators were welcoming and comforting. The people there knew what I was going through because they were or had been in the same situation. It was the one place I could go where I didn't feel as if I had to "put on a face" to demonstrate that I was okay. At the group meeting I could cry, talk about how hard it was to keep going, wonder if anyone ever got over the pain, compare struggles, find solutions, and listen to various experts on grief issues.

Sometimes we even laughed. I know that sounds strange, but sometimes when things are so bad, laughter is the only emotion that relieves the pain. Also, one of the facilitators made the best desserts, which were always an excuse to attend, even when I didn't feel like leaving my home.

During our time together, Jim and I had always shared a deep love of God and prayed together daily. When Jim died, my faith seemed to die also. How could God allow Jim to die, especially so young, when both of us had been so faithful? I struggled with this issue and am just now starting to feel some serenity. The group facilitators went out of their way to help me with this issue. I'm always amazed at how sharing feelings with others can soften the agony. Nothing totally eases the pain, but there is an amazing amount of wisdom among group members.

When I first started to attend the grief group, I attended faithfully. I am doing somewhat better in my daily life; I don't cry as often, my energy is closer to normal, and I'm learning to be just me, not half of a team. Now I just show up for group when I need a recharge. From time to time, I still struggle with grief symptoms: aloneness (that empty feeling of separation); the desire to share my feelings with my mate; and the longing to be hugged. Even though I don't cry as much, there is still that sadness deep within my soul. I'm told that too will pass. I wait for that day.

I would suggest that all people going through the throes of loss of a significant loved one find a group such as the Grief Coalition I attend. I am very thankful that this group was available to help me.

I Only Grieve When

I only grieve when I first wake
And strain to hear the sound
Of shower flow or dresser drawers
Bang shut as you move around

I only grieve when I come home
And you're not standing there
Or sitting where you used to be
To reach and stroke my hair

I only grieve when I don't hear
Your voice so low, so strong
Not saying much but speaking truths
That I so counted on

I only grieve when nighttime comes
And sleeplessness begins
I only grieve when I breathe out
And when I breathe back in

—Kathy Niebur

Phyllis

VERN GUERTIN

For a number of years, my wife, Phyllis, had suffered from bad health, including acid reflux, ulcers, and gall bladder and stomach problems. Her health deteriorated, and I felt it was best to retire to be home with her.

We made numerous doctor appointments trying to find some reason for her declining health. During one such test for stomach and colon problems, the doctor found a growth on her esophagus. He took one look at the tissue and knew it was cancer. Appointments were made to begin chemotherapy and radiation treatments. The prognosis was not good, and there was no guarantee either of those treatments would prolong her life.

Phyllis, however, refused treatment. "I've had a long, good life," she told me. "The children are grown and doing well. These treatments will diminish my quality of life, and I see no point in proceeding with them if I can't enjoy life with my children." While it was difficult to accept her decision, the children and I knew that once she made up her mind, it wasn't going to change. So we agreed to support her and do whatever we could, hoping to keep her comfortable and free of pain.

About six months after the diagnosis, her condition worsened and she now agreed to have hospice helpers. It was a good choice. Nurse Nancy was a wonderful, knowledgeable, and caring supporter who became a friend. Phyllis was always happy when Nancy came to the house.

As for me, I was in denial during her illness. I never believed she would die. It was so difficult to accept the reality. For weeks I felt discouraged, disconnected, and as if I were walking around in a fog. Eventually, Nurse Nancy was the one who helped me see the truth. I started using my spare time on repair and remodeling projects Phyllis had wanted done around the house for so long. It made me feel good knowing I had made her happy.

Any time we talked of death and dying, Phyllis would say, "Don't plan any kind of service for me, no open casket, no visitors, just put me in the ground." I was glad that Nurse Nancy was able to change her mind about that by helping her to see that a funeral was important for the family.

During those last weeks, Phyllis and I talked many evenings into the early morning hours. She shared her soul with me, relating things I'd never known about her during our forty-two years of marriage. We had an opportunity to make right any wrongs between us. Those long talks are now wonderful memories.

One morning she was having a good conversation, laughing with our daughter, Sue, before she left to go to work. It was so good to hear Phyllis laugh. A little while later, I went to check on her and found her lying on the bed with her legs hanging off the side. As soon as I lifted her legs to straighten her on the bed, and heard her very raspy and shallow breathing, I knew she was not in a good way. I immediately called the children and Nurse Nancy to come. "Phyllis's body is shutting down," Nurse Nancy said. "It could be hours, or maybe as many as three days, for her to die."

Listening to Phyllis's harsh breathing was so difficult. I didn't want her to just lie there and suffer for days. "Please, God, do something for her," I prayed. Then the children arrived, and I left the room for a few minutes. Phyllis died during those few minutes. (Later, I felt so guilty because I had not been there for the end of her life, and it would take me quite awhile to get over that guilt.)

In the end, Phyllis died thirteen months after her diagnosis. It was the children who planned the service and our son-in-law who gave the eulogy. There are blank spaces in my memory over those first few days. There seemed to be so many useless, trivial questions that I couldn't answer.

Feeling confused and disoriented, I thought I was losing my mind. At times I couldn't remember where I was or how I got there. I did find some relief by going for long walks, but I knew I needed help. The funeral director suggested I attend a grief group that would begin in nearby Cottage Grove in a few days. For six weeks after Phyllis's death, I attended that group. It was extremely helpful, and I was not ready for it to end. I learned of another group that met in Hastings once a week. The very next week I joined the Hastings group and continued attending for over a year.

I don't know where I would be today if it were not for each of these groups. Both were positive experiences. Being with others who knew how I was feeling and being able to share our stories was healing to me. I learned to treasure my memories, good and bad. Oftentimes, it was the bad memories that helped me to grow. Every week I left with some little tidbit from the educational speakers, and these helps stayed with me for days.

For example, I learned it was necessary to begin to create my own life apart from Phyllis. "New norms" they called this. We were told that our grief feelings would come and go for quite awhile. Knowing that was helpful. Because I cry for no reason, or I just sit in a chair and stare off into space. I was afraid I was regressing rather than progressing. I learned that grief healing takes work, and it is a process that doesn't just happen overnight.

On the first anniversary of Phyllis's death, my children and I were able to share our memories of her in a positive light. We got together for a pizza party, and lit the memorial candle that we bring out only on special occasions. These occasions become a part of the healing process.

I've met a lady friend who also has lost her significant partner. It's helpful to share our hurts and losses, and to have company to fill the lonely hours. We are helping each other become better persons and are growing stronger from our grief.

One of the grief group speakers talked about writing
her thoughts and feelings in a journal after her husband died
and how helpful that was. I took her suggestion and began to write
letters to my wife. Then I took the letters to the cemetery and read
them out loud to her. This was helpful for me.
I was able to express my pain, tell her my fears, my sorrows,
my regrets, and how much I love and miss her.

—Doug

"Make It a Great Day"

―

MIKE JUDGE

On December 12, 2002, my wife, JoAnn, had surgery at the University of Minnesota for a growth on her right lung. After three very long hours, the doctor came and told me the lump was cancerous.

For a while, the cancer was in check, but soon we were to find out there were also cancerous spots on both kidneys and in her spine. By January 2005 the cancer had spread to JoAnn's brain and, by March, to her liver.

We asked for a referral to Mayo Clinic in Rochester. Within a few days we were told by the doctors at Mayo that they agreed with the doctors at the University of Minnesota. I believe this was the day JoAnn gave up her fight. We came home and sat on the couch, and it seemed like we cried and held each other for hours. After that there were no more smiles.

As the caregiver during the last two and a half years of our lives together, I was willing to do anything for her. I soon found it was best to be prepared for a different experience every day. There were good days, okay days, bad days, and really bad days. Being a caregiver required a mental state somewhere in the middle, because the big swings wore very heavily on me and I couldn't afford to burn out. JoAnn told me many times that I was the one who was always positive, telling her that we were going to beat this and we were going to receive the miracle we had been praying for from the start. Her thanks and praise was a big plus for both of us.

To watch the person you have loved with every part of yourself for over thirty-three years endure pain and suffering is an experience too difficult for words. I can only say that the pain JoAnn suffered was more than anyone could ever have imagined. The cancer was very aggressive. JoAnn's fight ended with me sitting at the side of a hospital bed and holding her hand just as I had done so often over the previous six months.

Now she was gone and I found that, no matter how much I thought I had prepared myself for her death, my pain was beyond description. I could never explain what the death of a spouse is like. It simply cannot be put into words; only one who has undergone it can understand it. This was the first time in my life when I truly experienced feeling a shattered heart. Under the pressure of pain and loneliness, my body and mind became totally numb.

In the first few days after JoAnn had passed away, I was in such shock and so busy making funeral arrangements that I didn't have time to acknowledge any feelings. It was the afternoon after the funeral when I came home and the kids were not around that the grieving process began. When I walked into our house and noticed immediately how quiet it was, I had a total mental and physical collapse. I will never forget those two hours. They were by far the worst hours I have ever lived through in my lifetime. My feelings and emotions were totally out of control. The strongest feelings were that my life was completely over. I begged God to please bring me home so I could be with JoAnn. I thought the pain of her death was more than I could handle.

Picturing JoAnn in her coffin, I remembered how cold she always was, and I wondered if I should have put warmer clothes on her. I pictured the men at the cemetery throwing dirt on the person

I loved so much and had spent all of my life with since high school. Even though I knew she was already in heaven and that the body in that grave was not JoAnn anymore, it didn't seem to help.

I was so confused in the beginning that I had a hard time just getting through what used to be a normal day. I actually thought I was having mental problems. These emotions lasted for days and days until I realized that I needed to pull myself together and try to go on. For the sake of the rest of my family, I would be as strong as I could in front of them, while hiding my true feelings until I could be alone.

I went to JoAnn's gravesite at least once every day to talk to her, and I would ask her to pray for me because I really needed strength and guidance. I would also fill her in on how the family was doing, telling her about our boys (Jeff, Nick, and Ryan) and Ryan's wife, Jamie, and little Hannah, our granddaughter. That seemed to help. I also went to my doctor, and he put me on a couple of medications to help through the toughest times. The medications didn't take away the pain, but they did help me deal with my anxiety. My doctor also told me about other forms of help available and recommended I choose one or more.

Looking back, I see that the biggest, the hardest, and the worst feeling by far was the loneliness. I sat and looked to the future and didn't see anything out there but a big empty field. From being a husband, a provider, a protector, and a caregiver, I'd gone to being a nothing. No one to talk to, no one to eat with, no one to sleep with, and no one to share a good day or a bad day with.

I started to notice that most of the people who were our friends and who were always coming around before JoAnn died now stopped coming or calling. That added to the loneliness. I felt as if no one really cared about me. Later I learned that it was too hard for some people to call or stop over because we were all grieving, each of us in our own way.

I would always be so thankful when one of my sisters-in-law would call. One sister-in-law and I went out every Wednesday night for supper until she moved away; another invited me to go up north with her family. These things were huge, given my situation. I now so looked forward to things that were once just okay, such as a birthday party or a retirement party.

The one friend who didn't leave me was Jesus. I never lost trust in Him, nor did I ever get angry with Him. I just kept praying that He would give me the strength to get through. I don't know how many nights I would sit, so full of emotion and feeling as if I were the loneliest person in the world, but He gave me the strength to get up and somehow fight through another day. Sometimes I felt I was leaning on Him too heavily, because there were times when He was the only one I had to lean on. "If I lost Him," I thought, "I don't know what I would do." This is a time when my faith was really put to the test.

It was during one of these nights, sitting alone, that I realized I needed help to regain control of my life. I remembered that, in the packet I had received from the funeral home, was a brochure that talked about a Grief Coalition group that met in town. I decided I would give it a try.

That turned out to be the best decision I had made in a long time. The very first night I went, the speaker talked about how, in the beginning stage of grieving, you may feel as if you are going crazy. "Wow, that is exactly how I'm feeling," I thought. I started to learn that the grieving process is very similar for everyone. We all have the same feelings; the only difference between individuals is how each of us chooses to deal with these feelings.

I have not missed one Grief Coalition meeting since I started going to that Thursday night group. This is where I can talk about my experience, and I can hear others describe how they learned to deal with their grief experience. A special speaker every week addresses different parts of the grieving process. I highly recommend participating in such a group to anyone grieving a loss, whether of a child, a parent, or any loved one.

When JoAnn died that night, a part of me died, too. I hope that part of me went to heaven with her. I know I will never totally recover from losing her. People say it gets easier, that the pain will become less over time. One thing I know for sure is that my love for JoAnn will never lessen. JoAnn was truly the love of my life. I thank God for the three-plus decades He gave me with JoAnn. We had many wonderful times together and I will cherish those forever. It's my goal to enable her favorite saying, "Make it a great day," to come alive every day.

Thank you, JoAnn, for helping me to write this, just as you have always helped me.

I Thought I Was Getting Better

LINDA LUND

Life was good as my husband, Stan, and I approached the summer of 2000. My ministry was going well. Our daughter was married and had a good teaching job. We were preparing for the wedding of our son. Little did I know that my life was about to change.

Early in the morning of August 11, 2000, I awoke to discover myself alone in our king-sized bed. A little aggravated, I thought that Stan had fallen asleep in the recliner again. When I went downstairs to wake him, however, I knew immediately something was wrong. Stan was on the floor in a very strange position. Why didn't he answer when I called his name? I kneeled down beside him and took his hand—it was so cold. I remember screaming, and shaking him, and commanding him to wake up.

My world, as I knew it, was shattered. I went through the next days as if in a fog. I knew there were things to be done, decisions to be made, and people to notify, but I couldn't function. My children made most of the funeral arrangements.

The night of the visitation was extremely difficult, as I tried to greet every one of the seven hundred people who came through. I somehow made it through the funeral the following day, too.

The next few months were a blur. I didn't care about anything, and didn't want to do anything, go anywhere, or see anyone. The pain was physical and at times seemed unbearable. Unable to sleep or eat well, I kept thinking each day would get better. Finally, I took a medical leave from work and began to see a therapist. Although excruciating pain continued, I thought I was getting better.

In November my doctor insisted that I try antidepressants. I made it through Christmas and New Year's, Stan's birthday, our son's birthday, my birthday, and our anniversary. I thought I was on the mend and went back to work in January. Everyone was relieved.

But nobody around me had any idea of the pain and agony I was still experiencing. For months I muddled through work, putting on a smiling face for everyone, but not functioning normally. Although my doctor twice increased the dosage of my antidepressants, I slid deeper and deeper into depression.

A September 2001 breakfast with friends seemed to be the last straw. I couldn't handle their happy chatter! When I left, I got in my car and started driving through screams and tears. I just wanted to die and began planning how to accomplish it. Fortunately, God intervened, in the form of my son standing in my driveway when I arrived home.

It was at this point that I decided to enter a hospital program for depression. I also called my therapist and reestablished a connection with him. This time, when I requested a leave from my position at the church and applied for medical disability, my congregation, family, and friends were shocked. Everyone had thought I was doing so well. I will forever regret not being open with those who cared about me.

For the first six weeks of treatment, I participated in what is called a "Partial Program," an inpatient program where I went home at night and on the weekends. I then graduated to an outpatient program. Through this treatment, I learned so much about myself, and about depression and grief. While I was mad at God for taking Stan away, God still loved me and I truly believe His divine intervention is why I am alive today.

The journey has been a rough one. Stan's death threw me off a high cliff into what seemed like a bottomless pit of total despair. The climb back up from that pit has been long and difficult, but today I can say that I once again find joy in life. A pastor friend of mine likened my experience to Jacob's wrestling with the angel of God (Genesis 32:22). Jacob prevailed and in the end God blessed him, but Jacob was forever changed and went through the rest of his life with a slight limp.

Within six months of Stan's death two of my sisters also lost their husbands. While each of us has walked our journey of despair differently, and all three of us walk with that slight limp, each of us now has a stronger faith in God. We know that God was with us when we walked the darkest journeys of our lives.

Thanks be to God, the sun is out again, there is a rainbow in the sky, and life is, once again, good!

My Wounded Spirit

PAM MEYER

My husband, Kirk, and I met later in life on a cross-country ski trip along the North Shore of Lake Superior. We both also biked and canoed in the summer, and as our relationship grew, so did our mutual love of outdoor silent sports. We developed a strong emotional bond because Kirk had just lost a sister to cancer and my father was in treatment for cancer at the time we met. That led to some interesting discussions about life and death and our shared faith in God. Kirk was a very traditional Catholic, and I was a Protestant recently returned to my faith. Even with our differences, we respected and shared each other's faith.

We married in September 1997, two years after we first met. Our honeymoon was a bike ride across Arizona amidst the splendor of the Grand Canyon and the desert. Each following September, we headed up to the North Shore of Lake Superior with canoe and packs for a fall adventure in the Boundary Waters Canoe Area. It was a beautiful time of year to experience the quiet of the North Country, and to reflect and renew our spirits.

Our life was full of fun and full of promise. Then, in July of 2000, Kirk died suddenly but peacefully in his sleep. I was utterly and completely shocked. How could this be? In the few days prior to his death, we had biked seventy-five miles one day and forty-five miles another. Although Kirk had been diagnosed with cardiomyopathy seven years earlier, he was taking medications and seemed physically well. His death couldn't have been a greater surprise.

I remember sitting on my sunny deck the morning of his death, writing in my journal. The peaceful woods outside my door stood in stark contrast to my shocked grief as my thoughts rambled and I poured out my heart in words that hardly made sense. I questioned *why* God would take Kirk so suddenly after we'd had such a short time together. There was so much unfinished love and life to share. It seemed so unfair!

In the months that followed I felt deep despair and loneliness. My spirit was wounded and my body ached. I had difficulty sleeping and finally realized I needed a mild sedative to get good rest. I couldn't concentrate or even read a newspaper as my mind raced from one thing to another. I did find comfort in a daily meditation book, specifically for grieving widows, given to me by another widow. The book seemed to acknowledge what I was feeling many days. As I did that first morning of Kirk's death, I continued to journal through my pilgrimage of grief. My journal was and is a private place to express my grief, and the words seem to flow easily.

As the days passed, family and friends made suggestions as to what they thought would help me. While their intentions were sincere, they really did not know how I felt or what I knew was best for me. Grieving may be somewhat selfish, since at times it was best to decline uncomfortable situations, celebrations, invitations, or being with others who were not comfortable with my pain. Taking self-nurturing action felt good, as did surrounding myself with others who brought me comfort on unconditional terms.

I found that in grieving, "doing well" meant it was okay to have sad days, confused days, lethargic days, or nonproductive days. Finally, almost imperceptibly, life began to feel better again. I began to smile and laugh—laughter is so good for the spirit! I was able to complete tasks, especially all the business following death. I could read a novel again. When I began to pray, I once more felt God's presence in my life. Exercise, especially outdoors, brought me a sense of peace, and I found that the beauty of nature healed my wounded spirit.

Joining a grief support group was an important step in my grief journey. I attended my first Grief Coalition meeting in Hastings three months after Kirk's death. My sister, visiting from Colorado, accompanied me, which made it much easier to take that step. At the meeting I tried to speak, but was overwhelmed with tears and sadness, so I just listened. It was so comforting to hear that others felt the same pain. Over the next year, the grief group became my lifeline. It was a wonderful resource of speakers who shared their stories of loss. God carried me through those sad, dark days and brought me to a place where I was asked to share my story of grief and how my faith had comforted me.

As time went on my grief began to change. Earlier, I had questioned why God would take Kirk so suddenly. Although I felt angry, I knew the pain and hurt were too great for me to bear alone and that God was giving me the strength for each day. I acknowledged that grieving is a lifetime process—and the greater our love, the deeper the pain.

Since we never stop loving someone, we never stop grieving for him or her, either. With time, however, grief does change, and it becomes less painful. We start to see hope for new beginnings and we celebrate the life and blessings we shared with our loved one. I have come to recognize the gifts Kirk's life gave me during our short time together and I continue to celebrate his life with friends and family.

As I continue this journey of grief five years after Kirk's death, my life has taken on a much different direction from what I might ever have imagined. I have a whole new group of friends. I have survived cancer. I have biked to the top of two mountains, celebrating at the top all Kirk taught me, and praising the Lord on the way back down. I continue to share my story at Grief Coalition meetings and share in the grief ministry at my church. I feel my faith is at an all-time high, and I am grateful for the blessings I experience each day.

I know that with faith comes hope, trust, and comfort. I also know that God does not promise a life without pain and loss, but God does promise to comfort us and to be with us always.

I didn't lose my husband all at once on that day he died;
I lost him in little pieces every day. For instance,
when the lawn needs to be mowed and he's not here.
When the car wouldn't start.
When the garage needs cleaning—now I have to decide
what to do with all those tools.
The reality of my loss becomes more clear
with each reminder that he's not available in the here and now.

—Kathy

He Lived Life to the Fullest

JUDY MITCHELL

Ed, my husband, my best friend, my soul mate, and my hero, fought a very courageous battle against a rare type of cancer and won his victory on September 28, 2001.

When the cancer was first diagnosed in July 1997, Ed took on the news of cancer and was ready for battle. I, on the other hand, did not want to believe that this was happening to us, and was in a state of shock and denial. Why Ed?

Ed was expected to live a year to a year and a half, but God's mercy and grace took over and gave us four more years together. I became Ed's caregiver, finding an endless energy that could only have come from God.

Hospice came into our lives in May of 2001. Ed and I had talked about whether to stay at the house or to go to a hospice facility, and we chose to stay home. I was at Ed's side when he took his last breath. I knew he was dying, but I also had hope for a miracle. Was I still in denial? I don't know.

After Ed's "celebration of life" service, his mom, brothers, and sisters left my home. My mother-in-law thought that I should have time to myself, but that really wasn't what I wanted or needed at that time. I remember feeling very sad and alone.

Physically, I was exhausted, and as the days passed, all I wanted to do was sleep. Our two dogs were the main reason I got up in the morning. I was in a state of depression and felt totally numb. I didn't even know how to pray anymore.

Returning to our church was extremely difficult. No more sitting in the pew next to Ed, holding hands, being a couple. However, everyone in the church family was so loving; they wrapped me up in their love and made me feel so welcome.

About three weeks after Ed died, I felt like I was going crazy and I needed help; I needed some answers. I took a big step and attended the grief group that was meeting in Hastings, Minnesota. It was so scary to walk into a room of strangers.

Newcomers to the meeting were told, "Congratulations for making the first step into processing your grief." However, when you are so new to this process, you might walk away from a meeting with just a snippet of helpful information, because that's all that penetrated the numbness you are experiencing from the death of your loved one. I find that, as many times as I have returned to this group, I continue to learn more about dealing with my grief.

One thing that seemed to help me was buying a decorative candleholder and lighting this candle in memory of Ed and of other loved ones in my family who have passed on. I take this candle with me to a relative's home for Thanksgiving, Christmas, or Easter. Lighting the candle gives me a warm and comfortable feeling, almost to the point of sensing Ed near me.

Ed and I were blessed beyond measure during his battle with cancer, and these blessings were all in the name of Jesus Christ, our Lord and Savior. We had a very strong faith in Jesus, and I believe that is what got us through the very difficult times of living with and fighting the cancer. My faith in Jesus, the mainstay of my grief process, continually grows. I don't know how others get through such a huge loss without Jesus in their lives.

This past July, I served as a leader at a one-week camp for

middle school students. We had a new topic every day that some-one would talk about. Monday, I shared Ed's and my faith story. It wasn't easy to bring up these feelings again, but it proved to be another step toward my recovery. Thursday, the talk was on for-giveness, and we had to write a letter to someone in our life who we needed to forgive. I wrote my letter to Ed. When I was finished with it, I was emotionally spent. We then brought our letters to campfire that evening, and tossed them into the fire—another step to recovery.

I'm also working on a scrapbook of our life together. Yes, it hurts to look at pictures of us and see the things we did together. And yes, it hurts to find all the cards and notes he wrote to me and to read them and relive those times. Still, I'm so very grateful that I do have all those shared memories.

Strangely enough, when I feel in a really down mood I watch a sad movie. I bawl like a baby, even to the point of giving myself a headache, but I feel much better after my crying jag.

At the four-year mark of Ed's death, I was invited out to din-ner with my best friend from high school and her husband. It was a good evening. We talked about old times and I could even share with them about Ed. Although I dreaded this day, I tried to have something planned to look forward to.

Now, over four years since Ed passed away, I still have mo-ments that my aching heart misses him terribly. Nevertheless, I love to talk about Ed and I love to hear others talk about him, too. When they do, I say to myself, "Yes, they still remember him!"

Although I'm still working on my grief process, I am now one of the facilitators of the Hastings grief group that was so helpful to me, and I pray that sharing my story might give hope to others recovering from their grief. I encourage everyone who has lost a precious companion to be courageous and attend a grief group in his or her area. It's a club that no one wants to join, but anyone who does won't regret taking that first step.

Pretending

ROSE ROSS

The October autumn morning was cool and crisp. I had taken my daughters (ten and three years of age) to their dance lessons. When I returned home, I saw a note on the center island from my husband, Wayne. He and our son Nick had gone to hunt grouse on the land adjacent to our property. Nick had just turned twelve, and his dad was pretty keyed up to get him hunting more.

While I was cleaning upstairs, the doorbell rang and I nonchalantly walked down the hallway, unaware why there were such loud, urgent bangs on the locked front door. Then, through the glass pane of the door, I saw Nick in his blaze orange jacket. He was covered in blood and desperately screaming for me to open the door. Dennis, our neighboring farmer, was also standing with Nick. I had barely unlocked the door before Nick barreled through, shouting in pain and agony that he had killed his father with a stray bullet. "No," I said, "that can't be true!" But Dennis confirmed that it was. Wayne, my husband of thirteen years, was indeed gone.

Following Wayne's death, I insisted on carrying on with our daily schedules. Losing a father was a colossal change in the lives of our three young children. I couldn't bear to have them experience more changes that would upset their structured and smooth-flowing little lives.

Due to my insistence on living life as it had once been, I neglected to seek out the help and support that I myself needed. I did attend one session of the local grief group, but wasn't yet ready to be the "new widow" of the bunch. Instead, I felt that I needed to be certain that my children were cared for, and that they were healing and moving on.

Our scheduled life continued with schoolwork and extracurricular activities. I quickly returned to teaching. I also felt that it was important for all of us to continue to go to church. However, while we were still seen at mass each Sunday, getting the children to church became a battle. They reminded me that they "got nothing out of it," and would sit with their eyes closed during the service to catch a little nap. I wondered if this was their way of rebelling against God for taking their father away.

About a year and a half later I finally realized I could no longer single-handedly maintain the household, the children, and my own well-being. I needed some help. I began to attend grief group sessions again and also met privately with the leader of the group. She listened and watched as I cried and then cried some more. I began to feel as though my body were cleansing itself of the stress and worries I had been experiencing.

Also, I acknowledged that change was needed in our family, especially in our church life. The children and I sat down to discuss church, religion, and moving on. The children once again expressed their near loathing of church and religion. My son, Nick, claimed to be an atheist, and stated that he no longer needed to attend. However, I refused to believe they were truly anti-religious. Eventually, we agreed to seek out other churches to see if there would be one they liked better. We visited many new churches and more than one actually intrigued them, to the point that we engaged in good conversations on the way home. I felt hope strengthening in me.

After a year of searching, the children and I agreed upon a church. Since that time, our church has done more than I could have ever expected. All three children are involved of their own free will in the many programs it offers. Even Nick (formerly the self-proclaimed atheist) is now a youth group leader and a church camp counselor. Not only has he spoken twice at services, he has expressed an interest in becoming a pastor some day.

Finding common ground to share our faith in God has once again united us as a family. While the children don't know why their father had to die so young, they are more comfortable knowing he is in God's hands. We may hit some pretty big road bumps and potholes in life, but now we all agree that having faith in God can get us through anything.

Death of a Parent

My Mother, Myrtis Margaret Horkey

RUTH SYKORA

Our family consisted of my dad, mom, and four girls; that was the year when both my dad and my handicapped sister (age twenty-nine) passed away. Then, three years later, in an incredible and unbelievable instant in time, my mom was gone too.

December 17, 1999, dawned a beautiful, crisp, and sunny winter day. Mom was on her way to my home in Hastings, Minnesota, to pick up her sister. For some reason she was on a wrong road. We wonder if she was daydreaming and turned onto this road by mistake, because it was not the normal route she had taken so many times before. Rumble strips on the road warned of a stop sign ahead, but Mom ran through the stop sign and was hit broadside by a large truck. She was killed instantly.

Having already lost our dad and sister, we struggled to understand why this had to happen to our mom. She was in wonderful health and only sixty-eight years old. Mom was the one we expected to live to be a hundred, just like her father.

At first I was in a state of shock. I had a very difficult time believing that this had really happened to my mom. I remember walking down the streets in our hometown, going to various places to help prepare for her funeral. I couldn't understand why the world didn't stop because I was in grief! How can people simply go about their daily lives when my entire family is grieving so much? Doesn't anyone know I am grieving? Doesn't it matter to them?

I would lie awake at night, trying to comprehend what had happened. It was especially difficult to explain their grandma's death to my children (then fifteen, thirteen, and eleven). Some days I would cry and cry, and I didn't think I would ever stop. Then when I went a few days and didn't cry, I felt guilty for not crying.

During the period following Mom's death, my faith is what held me together and gave me the strength I needed. I clung to the memories of how Mom loved the Lord and how this love was very evident in her life. Up until the day she died, she was continually helping those in need. She would bring elderly friends to medical appointments, or clean their houses, or go to the grocery store for them. She would even stop to have a cup of coffee with them. The last few years of her life, she made it a practice to call each of us children and pray with us over the phone. This is something we especially miss.

During her visitation and funeral we heard many stories from people she had helped in the past. We derived such comfort from hearing these stories, and they gave us something to hang on to during the difficult days ahead.

Eventually, I attended a grief group. There, I learned that it is good to share your loss with others who have lost a loved one. Still, I think it's important not to let anyone else influence your grieving process. While we may not be sure our feelings are "right," we can't help how we feel. However, when we hear others talking about their grief, we find that our feelings are normal—there isn't a right or wrong to the feelings we have when we grieve. It's just that we all grieve differently and in different time frames.

Even though it seems as if Mom's death just happened yesterday, I have found that time does ease the grieving process. Yes, I will still have days when I cry for no reason, or when I hear a song she liked on the radio, or see a book she would have enjoyed read-ing. The special holidays—Mother's Day and Mom's birthday—are always difficult to get through. Christmas was one of her favorite holidays. We feel her presence when we attend Christmas events. It still makes me cry.

During these years, if I've learned anything at all it is how important it is to take each day one minute at a time. In addition, I also know how much it helps to rely on your family members and friends for support, even if it's just a hug.

Mourning Began with Bad News

CHRISTINE GARRICK

My mom died very young—she was only forty-eight years old. She had a difficult life, marrying and bearing me, her first child, at age fifteen. She was thirty-two years old and the mother of seven children. My father, an alcoholic, wasn't much help in raising our family.

Mom had diabetes and began to have great difficulty keeping it under control. She also had gone to the doctor complaining of chest and back pain. After numerous visits it was decided she needed heart surgery. But when they began the surgery, they discovered she had pancreatic cancer at a very advanced stage. One of my sisters called to let me know the findings.

My parents lived in Montana; I was attending college in Minnesota. I can remember driving home from class the night the results of Mother's biopsy were to come back from the lab. "If I died on the way home, I wouldn't have to face the results," I thought. That's when I realized my mourning had begun.

Mom took chemotherapy and radiation treatments, all to no avail. Often when I called my mom, she would be too weak or tired to come to the phone. My sisters called regularly to tell me how things were going. When Mom had good days, I would be filled with hope and thanksgiving. Then she'd have another bad day and the mourning would begin again.

During this time, I began to have nightmares of being buried alive and locked in small spaces, of my husband killing our son, of dead puppies and dead kittens hanging from trees. Every dream seemed to reflect death in some way or another. I guess it was always on my mind.

In the meantime, I went about my everyday activities—going to work and college classes, taking care of my two children, my husband and two dogs, as well as tending to my home and my garden. People would tell me how strong I was, and how well I was coping. Inside, though, I was screaming, "Can't you see my heart is breaking?" I couldn't believe people weren't able to tell how devastated I was. Ironically, the strength people told me they saw in me only made me push my feelings deeper. I think that may be why I had such terrible nightmares while Mom was ill.

I was with Mom during the last week of her life. No hospice services were available near our little mountain town, so her care rested solely with her family. When I couldn't bear to see her suffer any longer, I made the decision to have her taken to the hospital to die, even though she had expressed the wish to stay home. I carry some guilt because I made that decision.

In the end, Mom died less than a year after she was diagnosed with cancer. Her death brought many of my feelings to the surface. Guilt was foremost: guilt because of the decision I had made to hospitalize her; guilt because I was glad she had died, even though that was because she was no longer in pain; guilt because I was never truly close to her; guilt because I took her so for granted, sort of like the air I breathed; guilt because I didn't love her enough when she was alive. Before she died, I had never imagined losing my mother. I must have thought mothers were supposed to live forever; they're just *there*—even when you ignore them or don't think you need them any more.

Missing her was another of the feelings I had never allowed myself. Since we had not been close in either distance or relationship, I was amazed at how much I missed her now. I would think I was just fine—that I was finally over missing her—when all of a sudden I would remember that she was really gone and I would never see her again. It felt as if I had turned around and run into a brick wall. That sensation lasted for years and usually occurred when I was least expecting it. Then I would start crying and wouldn't be able to stop.

After many years, I dreamed she came to me and asked me what was wrong. I can still hear her voice saying, "Christy, what's the matter? Why are you crying?" I don't remember any more of the dream, but I do know that the pain of her death started to subside after that.

Where was my faith in all this? Always there, such a natural part of me that it was part of every breath I took. It helped me through all the busyness of her dying months and then facing life without her. Now, years later, her loss is still here with every breath I take.

"Our Dad, the Best"

―――

JENNIE MAHONEY and JAMIE NAWROCKI

My name is Jenny, and my sister's name is Jamie: this is the story about our dad, Jim Bennis, Jr.

My sister and I have been fortunate to grow up with two very loving parents. Even though our parents divorced during our adolescent years, my sister and I still remained extremely close with our dad. The three of us made it a priority to see each other as often as possible. We would go golfing, to a movie, hunting, to the cabin, or just have Sunday dinners at his house. We loved spending time together.

Dad was an inspiration not only to his family but also to friends and colleagues. He had been a hair salon owner for thirty years, touching the lives of many different people throughout that time. He was also active in Alcoholics Anonymous for sixteen years, helping people along the way. It was so easy for him to connect with many others. Our dad was loving and gentle, and had understanding like no other. We could talk to him about absolutely anything. Not only did he always give good advice without being judgmental, he also had a great sense of humor when we needed it most. Making each other laugh was one of our favorite things to do. Dad was the one person we could not imagine living without. He was always there when we needed him, and he seemed invincible to us.

Then, on September 20, 2004, we received news that would change our lives forever. Mom showed up at my home at 12:30 in the morning, along with my grandma and two aunts. I was totally startled and worried. She told me that something had just happened to my dad. "Is he okay?" I asked. "No," she said. "He's had a heart attack. He's gone." I have never been so shocked in all my life. I couldn't believe her. I fell to the floor and couldn't even cry. I could hardly breathe. The shock that went through my body was crushing; it was a feeling I had never experienced.

Then Mom helped me get dressed and told me we had to go and tell Jamie. Still in disbelief, I felt absolutely sick and green all the way to my sister's house. Of course, Jamie was extremely shocked when she saw us at the door in the middle of the night. She obviously knew that something very bad had happened. When Mom said, "It's Dad," Jamie replied, "Not my dad, you mean Grandpa, right?" Mom said, "No, it's your dad. He's had a heart attack."

Jamie reacted the same way I did, with total shock and disbelief. We sat up all night long because we couldn't sleep. When someone that you love dies suddenly, it shocks your whole system. You feel it physically. You can't eat or sleep, and everything in your body hurts. It truly feels like you have a broken heart.

Finally, the night blended into morning. By afternoon we were picking out a casket, still totally numb and shocked, just going through the motions. Amazingly, everyone else seemed to be carrying on as usual, while our world had stopped and all of the daily things in life seemed irrelevant to us. The numbness stayed with us throughout Dad's wake.

Seeing him for the first time after we knew he was gone was one of the hardest parts of the grieving process. It made his death very real to us. At the funeral home, we stood in the receiving line for five straight hours. A line of well-wishers formed early and wrapped around the funeral home and down the block. We were in awe to see how many people were there because Dad had touched their lives. It gave us a new outlook on why people have a wake for a loved one, and we felt proud and honored to have Dad as our father.

After a couple of days, reality began to sink in: this really did happen. Weighed down with emotions, we cried so much we didn't think it would ever stop. We couldn't believe we would never see our dad again. All sense of normalcy in our everyday life disappeared. Soon we started having questions and doubts about everything we had ever believed. Our faith was put to the test, and we didn't understand why God would suddenly take from us someone we loved so much.

Dad's faith in God, however, gives us comfort. In fact, just one week before Dad died, Jamie's husband had been given a homework assignment to ask people for their views on Christianity. This is what Dad wrote in response:

> To accept that Jesus is my Savior who came to die
> for our sins. And that He is the Son of God. And to live
> by His work, which is found in the Holy Bible. The Spirit
> of God was in Jesus, his Son. Believe that it's not about
> me, but God's grace to give me life. I should honor Him
> by following His work in my life.

How fortunate we are to have this witness to his faith. We soon realized that we, too, needed to put our trust in God. We prayed more than we ever had before, especially that God would give us peace and a sense of closeness to our dad. Knowing that he is in a better place and that we will see him again someday has kept us from becoming angry with God. We know in our hearts that God wouldn't take Dad just to hurt us.

We also asked God to help us both with the tremendous anxiety that came along with our grief. Nothing could have prepared us for the irrational and fearful thoughts that consumed our minds, even though we had a strong faith. We also experienced many physical anxieties, such as chest and stomach pains. As if we had gone through a major surgery, our bodies and minds needed a long time to heal.

Another part of the healing process for us was finding a grief support group in our community. The first time we went was hard; we didn't know what to expect. We soon found how comforting it was to be around people who understood our grief. There's just something about sharing with other people—even total strangers—the experience of having a loved one die. Those who haven't experienced such a loss don't know how to help in the same way.

The people at our grief group made us feel like we had a new network of support and friends. We also learned a lot about the grieving process, including that all of our feelings were normal. The speakers were always very informative and empathetic. We found that attending the group each week was one of the most important steps on our road to recovery. At one time we thought we would never feel okay again. Also, we didn't want to let go of the pain we felt from our loss, as we knew we would grieve for our father the rest of our lives. Then we learned that we don't have to let go, but it does get easier.

If anyone were to ask us how to get through grief, we would say this: forget about the usual anxieties of everyday life; take life one day at a time; and realize that we all grieve at a different pace. Before Dad died, we took a lot of things in life for granted. We never really grasped the concept that someone as dear to us as our dad could die. Now we understand how fragile life is.

A Grief Revisited

PEGGY ALSDURF

In ten minutes, my father went from drinking a glass of milk to rolling on the floor in pain. Even Novocain in Milk of Magnesia in the emergency room did not deaden the waves of pain that roared through his belly. Slowly at first they came, giving minutes of relief between episodes. Then faster, stronger, longer until he could no longer do anything more than survive each onslaught. The last coherent words I heard my father say came in a lull between the spasms. "Take me now, Jesus," he gasped. "I'm ready to go."

Pain gave way to fever as infection raged through his body. By the time it receded, the damage was done. Days of hopeful watching for signs of recovery stretched into a week; a week stretched into three. Hope faded as reality set in. Out of time now, decisions had to be made. Machines were turned off and we watched as the tide of life washed out of his face, bringing him peace at last.

What grief! But it was strangely mixed with relief. Dad's was a good death, a holy death. Needed words had been spoken, and reconciliations had occurred. Family had been restored. Is this what they call "good grief"? Then what do they call what happens next?

As the emotional anesthesia wore off, a different kind of grief emerged. The painful memories, his last days of suffering, the roller coaster of emotions in ICU, the unfairness and unreality of it all: "It's a dream," I thought. "He's just on a trip." But those "firsts" without him kept coming: the empty chair at Christmas, the birthday with no cake or candles, a Fourth of July family picnic.

Then, with the grief process barely begun, it was rudely interrupted. No, not Mom! But yes: symptoms persisted, tests analyzed, diagnosis given—terminal. This can't be happening! We can't lose Mom, too—not after losing Dad just fourteen months ago.

Grief for Dad is put on hold, and focus on Mom becomes paramount. Four months passed as we shared together, talking, crying, praying, preparing. I spent hours memorizing her face, listening to her words, hearing her heart, and asking all the questions that needed to be asked. "God is good," Mom said. "He never, ever makes mistakes. You can trust Him!"

Too soon one summer afternoon, my world stopped as Mom lay in bed gasping for breath. Her children stood at her side, helpless to do anything but hold her and love her. Then, surprisingly, calm came, and a smile slightly curved her lips as her gaze focused on a corner of the room. One more breath and then she gently slipped away. Another holy death. How can it hurt so much but seem so right?

All the pain comes flooding back, this familiar pain that makes me want to jump out of my skin, to go away somewhere and come back when it's over. Sleepless nights, pain-filled days, hearts ripped once more: how can I go through this again?

We were orphans now, with closets to empty, clothes to give away, belongings to divide, financial affairs to settle. And then the house—ah, the house, the last safe place of childhood. A sale, and then in a few days, nothing remains but bare walls and empty rooms—nothing but memories. And the next work of grief begins, the one that lasts a lifetime: learning to live without the ones you love.

So how am I doing, a year and a half later? The sharp pain has subsided. There are even days when I can smile at a funny memory. As the memories of illness and deathbeds fade, it is the memories of the little things that hurt. It is the ache of all the empty places, of missing Dad's crooked smile, Mom's chocolate chip cookies, his wise advice, her encouraging words, his dumb jokes, her singing in the kitchen, his strong hands building things, her comforting hands smoothing the tears away.

What helps? Prayer, sleep, support from friends, sharing the memories with brothers and sisters. Finding friends who care and listen. Meeting others who have gone this way before me. Listening to those newly grieving who come behind me, and sharing the comfort that I have received from the God of all comfort Himself.

Reading Scripture brings me peace. Acknowledging honestly where I am on this journey, not only to myself, but also to God, to my family, and to the friends I trust, keeps things in perspective. Praying for others helps; everybody carries his or her own load of pain. Attending a local grief support group of other folks who have lost those they love helps me to know that I am not alone and I am not crazy because I still grieve after all this time.

When the painful memories come, I have learned to push them away and replace them with memories of the good times. I reflect on the wonderful heritage my parents gave me, and I try to live so that they would be proud of me. And I remember that I will see them again someday when my time on earth is finished.

Even with all these things, I think I finally turned a corner emotionally when I began to intentionally cultivate a grateful heart. With so many things to be sad, mad, or depressed about, even in the hard times I can find something for which to be thankful. There will always be things in my life that are negative, unfair, pain-filled. If I concentrate on what I don't have, I will miss the wonderful joy of what I do have. And if I don't appreciate it now, I will be sorry when it is gone.

What else have I learned?

Life is temporary. Heaven is closer than you think. Not very much in life is really that important except people. And nothing helps like spilling everything out before the One who made you and hears you and knows you and loves you. My mom was right. Life is hard, but God is good and I can trust Him. He has a wonderful way of making something good out of even the most difficult experiences. I've seen it before; I will see it again.

Once we accept the fact that life is difficult,
that the mystery of why calamities and suffering occur
will never be fully solved on this earth, then and only then will we
stop demanding that a satisfactory answer be found and begin
to get on with life.

—Author unknown

Death of a Child

Our Firstborn

DONNA and RANDALL OVERSTREET

Karen was the firstborn of our three children. From the beginning, she was a determined child, upbeat and loving. As she grew up, she derived great joy from organizing family dinners and holiday celebrations, and Thanksgiving was always held at her house. She loved Christmas, too; a gift giver, she would begin shopping for the next Christmas as soon as the wrappings were cleaned up from the current one.

It was July of 2003 when Karen was diagnosed with skin cancer. She had four operations to remove cells; the operations and treatments were very painful. Then in November of 2004 she was diagnosed with an aggressive ovarian cancer (unrelated to the skin cancer). Treatments began immediately. She had received twenty-six radiation treatments, four sets of chemotherapy, and sixty-five hours of radium treatments between November 2004 and the middle of April 2005, when she made the decision to stop all treatments. Nothing seemed to be working to eradicate the cancer. She died shortly thereafter, on April 29, 2005.

Karen left behind her husband, Mark Norton, and three daughters. (Her firstborn, a son, had died of "crib death" at nine weeks of age.)

Donna, Karen's mother

I took care of Karen every day at her home so that her husband, Mark, could continue to work, doing what I could to make her comfortable and preparing food for her. Most days she spent lying on the couch, and she was losing weight fast because she was so sick she couldn't or wouldn't eat.

A day or so before she died, as Karen was trying to get to the bedroom, she lost her balance and fell, hurting her head. By this time I believe she knew her life was coming to an end. Perhaps she just gave up.

On April 28 we made arrangements for hospice. That was very difficult, because we felt as if we were giving up, that there was just nothing more to be done. I was so afraid we were losing her. That evening our pastor came to pray with her. Following the prayer, she opened her eyes and said "thank you" to him. Those were her last words. She died the next morning.

It seemed as if life stood still. I had things to do but couldn't do them. I had been so busy for all those months that I had put my own life on hold. Now with nothing to do for Karen, I was confused and numb. I could not get the *why, why, whys* to stop in my head. My body felt heavy, and I felt sure that the sadness was more than I could take. I had anxiety attacks and developed nervous shakes that are still with me. I am afraid that if I really start crying I will never be able to stop, and I have not been able to really cry yet. Sometimes the pressure is so heavy it causes my head to ache.

A few weeks after Karen's funeral, Randall and I went to the grief group that meets at the senior center in our community. We couldn't talk about Karen yet, but it was helpful to hear the stories from others. Listening to the speakers and others in grief, I realized I was not going crazy and the way I was feeling and thinking was part of the grief. It was very helpful. I remember one statement in particular: "Nothing will ever be normal again." That is so true.

Our lives as we knew them have changed, and we can never go back to the way they were.

Randall, Karen's father

Karen was a daddy's girl, and we enjoyed a close relationship. When she became ill and the diagnosis didn't look good, I wasn't sure I could survive without her. I still wish I had been the one to go, rather than my "little girl."

One day last February, Karen was resting and I went out for a walk—walking helps me deal with my stress level. On that walk I found a small child's stuffed Care Bear toy. I cleaned it up and took it to Karen. It stayed on the back of the couch, keeping her company, until the day she died.

I told Karen often that I loved her. On the night before she died, she was very weak and could hardly talk, so I thought I would get in the last word. I laid my hands over my heart and said, "I love you." With all the effort she could muster, she brought her hands to her heart and in a very soft, weak voice said, "I love you more." She gave the last "I love you."

Not long after Karen's death, my son and I were helping clean Highway 55, along with our church group, and we came across a child's picture with angels on it. Karen collected angels; they were special to her. Both of us felt that this little wrinkled picture was a sign that Karen was okay.

My sadness is always with me. I go to the cemetery about every day to talk to her. I have to take walks. I can't sleep, and I cry daily. The grief group was helpful, but I never got to the place where I could talk; it was just too painful. Even now, I still cry when I think of Karen or try to talk about her.

Donna and I do find comfort in small things. For example, Karen liked butterflies and redbirds. We have been amazed at how many butterflies come around our house, and there's a redbird that shows up just about every day. The grandchildren (eight grandchildren and nine great-grandchildren) are a blessing to us, too, and we spend a great deal of time with them.

Our church family has been the best of help for us, sending cards, bringing food, giving hugs, and making sure we're okay. A good, loving support system certainly helps with the grieving process. Our faith in God also keeps us going, as we know the Lord has strengthened and is strengthening us and is helping with our healing. We also know that Karen is in heaven and we will see her again. That is comforting.

As I think about it, it seems strange to me that all of my brothers and I have lost our firstborn child, and Karen had also lost her firstborn.

I am not sure what we will do for the holidays and Fourth of July celebrations. Karen always organized the celebration for us.

I miss her voice.

Anger Intensified

JIM BENNIS

I am no stranger to the loss of a loved one, or to the anger and sadness it has caused in my life. I believe it began at age eleven, when my father, just thirty-one years old, died of a heart condition. "You are now the head of our family, and you will need to be strong for your mother," I was told. I relied on my grandparents, who served as good role models for me, and I thought a lot of them. But their passing left another gaping hole in me.

At age eighteen, I got married; my wife and I had six children, five boys and one girl. When my wife died suddenly in 1990 of a heart attack, it was yet one more terrible shock to me.

Just two years later, in 1992, I lost my oldest child, Joe. Diagnosed with a brain tumor, he had surgery four days later. After the surgery, he had a stroke and had to be placed in a nursing home, where he lived until his death ten months later. To fight off the feelings of hurt and sadness, I became a very angry man.

Twelve years had passed when my son, Jim, Jr., died. It was September 2004. My current wife and I were headed to Idaho for a reunion with my brothers and sister. Back home, my son, Scott, and his wife were expecting a baby by caesarean section on September 20, and when I called home that day, we were happy to hear that the new baby boy, and his mom and dad, were all doing fine.

However, our happiness over a new grandson was all too quickly overshadowed. The next morning, as we were leaving Cut Bank, Montana, our phone rang. It was my brother calling to tell me that my son, Jim, Jr., had died of a heart attack on a hunting trip. We had lost a son and gained a grandson on the same day.

Numbness set in and I shut off my feelings for the two-day drive back home. I wasn't sure I could handle the grief along with the stress of driving, but God always helps me when I let Him. When I prayed, I could feel His spiritual support as I drove.

The first nine months after Jim's death were almost unbearable. I had attended a grief group when my first son died and received a great amount of help dealing with my feelings, so I knew they were normal and that I wasn't losing my mind. Yet I was still overwhelmed with dark feelings I couldn't really identify.

Already an angry person, I found that my anger intensified after Jim passed away. Some of my anger came from fear, and some of that is fear of losing another son or daughter. My counselor friend told me to think about turning my anger into sadness, and that process worked for me. It makes it easier on me and on those around me.

In addition to all the strong emotions I was feeling, I also suffered with a great deal of physical pain in my back and neck. Eventually, I needed a doctor's help to overcome the overwhelming physical and emotional pain. Losing my two oldest sons was more than I could handle on my own.

I'd like to say that my faith carried me through, but to be honest, faith is hard for me. Sometimes I feel as if I have a lot of faith and then at other times I feel as if it has left me. I know intellectually that things will get better and will work out if I just don't let the fear get in the way. But sometimes I simply "act as if" until my faith returns.

Looking back, I see that I wasn't really able to grieve until I went to a grief counselor when I was forty-seven years old. I also began to attend the local grief group each week. Working through my grief with the help of the leaders and other group participants has helped me immensely, especially as they shared their stories and the knowledge they had gained. Educational speakers and interaction with others also helped me.

I am very grateful for the support I have received, and I would recommend that anyone who has lost a loved one make an effort to attend a grief group. It is well worth the time and effort.

At first my grief followed me everywhere. It was
on my shoulder, in front of my eyes, in my heart and mind
all day. It consumed my days and my thoughts,
but as time went on, each little victory was a big step and now,
it's still there—it probably will always be with me—
but a new and deep joy is creeping in and
life is becoming good again.

—Carol Parrott,
author of Parents' Grief: Help and Understanding
after the Death of a Baby

Grief of a Mother

KAREN PRIBNOW

In 1976, five years after my marriage to Butch, a Minnesota dairy farmer, we adopted three-month-old Kristina. Four years later we adopted our son Troy, who was then eleven months old. We thought that our family was complete, until what seemed a miracle happened in the fall of 1986, when I learned that I was pregnant.

It was so exciting, but hard to believe, too. Every Sunday when I sang "Praise God from Whom All Blessings Flow," I thanked God for my unborn baby and prayed that she would be born healthy. My prayers were answered when our daughter Amy was born on April 16, 1987. At nine pounds, five ounces, she was definitely healthy!

A happy baby, Amy's eyes always showed a special sparkle, and she smiled a lot. She grew into a child with a curious mind, always wanting to know what was going on. As a teenager, Amy was concerned for our financial well-being, and when she was sixteen years old, she got a job and began to pay for her car insurance and clothes. She and I shared special shopping trips, talking and laughing together.

Then the unthinkable happened. Just sixteen years old, Amy was killed in a one-car accident on October 25, 2003. Ironically, of the six girls in the car, she was the only one wearing a seatbelt. The car hit the only tree in the ditch on Amy's side. Her neck was snapped and some of her teeth were knocked out.

For weeks I did not sleep well. Although I had been told that she did not suffer, thoughts of Amy kept returning to haunt me, and I cried often. "Why did God choose Amy?" I wondered so often. "Did I do my job and teach her about God? Did she go to heaven? What do I need to do to make sure that I join her?"

Then I started to question God's plan for me. Along with daily Bible reading, I also read *The Purpose Driven Life*, as well as other spiritual books. The new hygienist at the dentist office recommended a religious radio station that I listened to as I drove to and from work. I also used some of my drive time for prayers of gratitude and praise.

In the beginning, I think I cried every morning and every night. During this difficult time, I so appreciated the wonderful support of my family and my church family. Also, Amy's friends and some of their parents would tell me how she was a friend to so many, treating everyone as a special individual, and inviting newcomers to join in her group of friends. I believe that God sent these dear people to us. They provided support, a hug, a card, and a gift; most important of all, they listened to me talk about Amy.

To maintain our connection to Amy, Butch and I supported her friends by attending their school events. I came to understand how important it was to remember others who may also be in mourning and who needed our support. Instead of staying home and giving in to loneliness, I joined Big Brothers Big Sisters and became a mentor at a local school. I also become a Saturday mentor for another little girl.

My suggestion for others who are recovering from the loss of a child is to get involved with their church family and friends, and to talk about their loved one. This has helped me to accept that, yes, we are all going to die, some at an earlier age than others. However, we will be joined again in heaven if we follow God's Word. My faith in God has helped me during this time of tragedy.

Eventually, one and a half years passed after Amy's death, and I could begin to see an improvement in the way I felt. It had taken me that long before I could begin to sort through her personal belongings. I have gone through her closet, but I have left her pictures and personal items where I can see them, as I still enjoy the memories they bring to mind.

This weekend I found a couple of movies that I had not transferred to a video. In the movies, Amy was laughing and just being herself. What a wonderful blessing! I felt as if she had just visited me in person!

The Strength to Forgive

DONNA MATHIOWETZ

There was a knock at the door at 11 p.m. that foggy Friday night in March. I opened the door and recognized the deputy sheriff. He stepped in and introduced the woman with him as the county coroner. Our sixteen-year-old son, Timm, had been shot and killed by an acquaintance at a party. The combination of beer, poor judgment, and a handgun changed our lives forever. The minutes and hours that followed are still etched in my mind fourteen years later. At times it seems like yesterday, yet it's been such a long time since I've felt a hug from Timm's strong arms. One of my most vivid memories is of the short prayer that my husband, Dick, and I prayed early the following morning. It was a simple request asking God to take any destructive anger from our hearts. He did just that.

As the months went by, I had moments when I sensed being held in Jesus' arms. I understood He didn't choose this to happen, but I also recognized that He didn't stop it. Why . . . why? I spent some time, as most people who suffer a tragic loss do, asking this question. It didn't take long to realize that no one could answer it to my satisfaction.

Over time, God guided me to replace the "why?" with "what

now?" I had grasped on to and believed what Romans 8:28 tells us: "We know that in all things God works for the good of those who love Him, who have been called according to His purpose." God's purpose for my life began with baby steps, as I was able. The journey of grief is a marathon, not a sprint.

As I educated myself about this uninvited visitor in our lives I learned of the importance of taking care of myself mentally, spiritually, and physically. I had enjoyed walking before Timm's death and resumed it soon afterwards; it was a good way to relieve some of the stress I was experiencing. I often prayed as I walked and tried to listen for something from God. He caused me to begin to think more about the young man who shot Timm, as well as considering what his family might be experiencing. Then a few steps at a time God led me down a path called "forgiveness." After a few weeks my husband and I had the strength to forgive. The forgiveness came in three areas.

First we chose to forgive ourselves for anything we didn't do right as parents. Secondly, we forgave Timm for the lack of judgment he demonstrated that night. Then finally we chose to forgive the young man who shot him. I wrote him a letter while he was imprisoned to express our forgiveness. We didn't condone his actions, but we forgave him as God has numerous times forgiven us. Choosing to forgive enabled us to continue on our grief journey without the burdens of revenge or getting even. Because we chose to forgive, we have been able to use this life experience to be there for others as they face the same challenges.

Garth

RONALD KOCHER

On November 9, 1970, our firstborn son, Garth, died of acute blast cell leukemia; he was only fourteen years old.

During that summer of 1970, Garth had spent school vacation time mowing lawns and working two paper routes in Riceville, Iowa, our home at that time. He seemed to be tired a lot, but then he would rest and go back to his chores. During the last part of October, however, we grew more concerned, as he seemed to be getting ever more tired and weak each day. We scheduled an appointment at a medical clinic in Mason City, Iowa; after examination, the doctors told us that he had an upper respiratory infection. We took Garth home, but he didn't seem to improve.

On October 31, 1970, we drove Garth to Fayette, Iowa, to stay with his grandparents, and to attend a Halloween party at his former school. Along the way, we stopped at an eye doctor's office in West Union, and Garth almost fainted in the doctor's office. However, Garth really wanted to stay with his grandparents and attend the party, which he did. His grandparents brought him home on Sunday.

On Monday, November 2, we contacted our local doctor. After

examining Garth, the doctor was able to arrange an appointment at Mayo Clinic in Rochester, Minnesota, for the next day, Tuesday. Garth was admitted to St. Mary's Hospital for observation and tests. We returned the seventy-five miles home and asked my wife's parents to come and stay with our other three children so that we could make daily trips to Rochester.

Returning to the hospital at 6:00 a.m. on Wednesday, we observed the doctors doing a bone marrow exam on our son. At noon the doctors told us Garth had acute blast cell leukemia. They started Garth on a regimen of chemotherapy, which he pulled out in the middle of the night since he was in so much pain and didn't realize what he was doing. Several times I prayed that God would either heal our son or let me replace him, but God's plans were not my plans.

As we struggled through the next few days, we met some parents whose son was recovering from an appendectomy. This wonderful Jewish couple shared our stunned disbelief over what was happening to Garth. The Wednesday that we learned that Garth had leukemia, we were wondering where to stay in Rochester so we could always be close to him. This kind man said he owned some apartments and had just completely remodeled one after a fire. "You can use it as long as you need it," he said.

Then, on Monday, November 9, a couple of friends came to visit and asked to take us to dinner. Since our pastor and his wife from Riceville, Reverend and Mrs. Maurice Gunn, were also there and said they would sit with Garth, we agreed to go to dinner at the restaurant across the street. We had just reached the restaurant when Reverend Gunn arrived. He told us that Garth had suddenly sat up in bed and said, "Dad, Dad, I've got to tell you something." Then he lay back down. His brief life ended around 9:00 that evening, and I never learned what he had wanted to tell me.

(As a side note: some years earlier, Reverend and Mrs. Gunn's daughter was mauled and killed by a bear while camping, and they were not there when she died. Reverend Gunn told us later that it was a blessing to them to be with Garth when he died, as it helped provide closure in the loss of their daughter.)

After Garth's death, at first I was angry with the doctors who had not diagnosed the disease earlier, and then I was upset that a cure for his sickness was not available. I was also mad at myself for failing to provide a secure life for our son.

My sorrow before, during and after the funeral was devastating. However, as family, friends and neighbors talked to us, we heard stories from people whose lives had been touched by our son, and I came to realize that we are not alone in our grief. Instead, the Lord provides others to share in our sorrows and to provide support that in ways we may not even realize at the time.

As time passed, I know that I buried myself in my job, and I am sure that my family may have thought that I didn't care as much as others did, but men do try to hide their grief behind their work faces.

Today when I look at my children, grandchildren and great-grandchildren, I can't help but wonder what life would have been like if Garth had survived and had a family. I think of Garth often, and I always remember his last words: "Dad, Dad, I've got to tell you something."

It has been thirty-five years since Garth's death, but it seems just like yesterday. Still, Garth's last words always give me strength. I so look forward to the day that I can find out what that "something" was that Garth wanted me to know. Was Jesus there with him? Did God show him a new home? The day will come when I'll know the answers to these questions.

For now, I need to keep myself more focused on that day, and I need to do a better job of setting an example for my family and others, so they can believe that Jesus is the way. Sure, many men have a difficult time with grief, as I have. Yet I now know that I am not alone. Many are willing to sit with listen, and me and, of course, God and Jesus are just a prayer away.

A Million Times

A million times we've thought of you,
a million times we've cried.
If love alone could have saved you,
you never would have died.
In life we loved you dearly,
in death we love you still.
In our hearts you hold a place
no one could ever fill.
It broke our hearts to lose you,
but you didn't go alone.
For part of us went with you
that day God called you home.

—*Author unknown*

Pregnancy and
Infant Death

My Elora Grace

ANDREA HOWARD

With every smile I find my place
Deep within the heart of Elora Grace.
I close my eyes and dream your face
My world, my love, my everything—My Elora Grace
       Never have I seen such beauty
       Never have I felt such love.
       In the presence of an angel
       An unknown strength emerged in me.
       You will forever be my focus,
       An image of pure perfection,
       My world, my heart, my reason—My Elora Grace
              When the waves crash long and hard
              I will close my eyes and reach for you
              To feel those tiny fingers and not-so-tiny toes
              So kissable, so lovable, so unbelievable.
              With vivid color and perfect peace
              I see you safe in our Heavenly place
              Sweet Jesus to your left side
              And Great Grammy to your right.

I will lock my eyes on this every day to come
Every day one day closer to where my heart belongs
With my world, my path, my masterpiece—
My Elora Grace

Elora Grace Howard   "Elora": The Lord is my light
July 16, 2005   "Grace": God's kindness

No Remember Whens

ANDREA BARKER

All my life I've wanted a big family, and it seemed that my greatest fear was not being able to have children. Then my husband, Adam, and I were blessed with a beautiful baby girl nine months after we got married, and I thought having more children wouldn't be problem. However, my next two pregnancies resulted in miscarriage—one at about five weeks, and the other at ten weeks (a blighted ovum they called it). Although I was devastated with these two losses, my next pregnancy resulted in a live birth. I never forgot the two miscarriages, but I was happy I had two children.

After much debate, we decided to have a third child. I was elated when I finally got pregnant, and at the same time terrified that I might miscarry again. Every night I prayed and told God my fears.

I watched for signs of miscarriage, but there were none. Then I began to feel uneasy. A week later, at my first doctor's appointment, she had trouble hearing the baby's heartbeat. An ultrasound confirmed that the baby was dead. My baby had grown to ten weeks and five days, and then just stopped growing. Numbness settled in, and I felt as if I were in a fog. Adam and I stared out the window for that first week, and couldn't even talk about it.

I remember feeling so guilty and wondering what I had done to cause the miscarriage. The doctor said that it was probably a chromosome miscomputation, but what if it was something I did, such as playing kick the can with the kids, or having sex? I wondered if God thought I was a bad mother, and I got angry with Him.

Visions of dashed dreams—three little girls running and playing and snuggling up to me—mocked me, especially when lab tests confirmed that our baby was a perfect little girl who had nothing wrong with her chromosome makeup. We named her Jessica Lynn.

After a couple of weeks, family support begins to run out. No one asks how you are doing anymore. I think that the problem with miscarriage is that no one else is all that invested in it, and they don't understand the loss. With the death of a living person, there are memories for everyone to share. "Remember when . . ." With miscarriage, there are no "remember whens."

About three weeks after Jessica's death, I called the pregnancy and infant loss contact person at the hospital. After listening patiently, she referred me to the Hastings Area Grief Coalition group and said she would meet me there on Thursday. I was apprehensive about going to a group whose members had losses of all kinds. Would they understand the pain my miscarriage had caused? Would they welcome me? Would they all be old people? What if some there had lost babies and could never have other children? Would they say, "You should be happy, at least you have two healthy children"?

As it turned out, the people at the grief group were very receptive to me. I also met with the pastor and the pregnancy and infant loss contact after the first session. Their listening to me and validating my feelings helped immensely. "In fact," they said, "you are a mother of four!" That was the most helpful encouragement to me. Yes, I am a mother of four. It's just that two of my babies are in heaven.

When they learned that I was so upset about not having three children for the upcoming Christmas, they told me that there was no reason I couldn't have a stocking for the baby. I also made a memory card for her, as well as memory boxes with the few keepsakes I had, and I plan to make a memory book, too. I purchased tree ornaments with all three of the girls' names, and when her sisters Ellie and Molly are old enough, these ornaments will remind us all of Jessica whenever we decorate a Christmas tree. Finally, I am going to buy the Christmas present that I would have gotten for Jessica and donate it in her memory.

I love Jessica. She will always live in my heart, and I know we will meet again.

Daniel's Story

JEANNETTE SINDT

In March of 1992 I experienced the death of my second son, Daniel. He was stillborn. I had spent eleven weeks on bed rest and medications to prevent this baby from being born early. Over and over I was told that the longer I could delay delivery, the better chance my baby had of surviving. At thirty-seven weeks of pregnancy, however, my doctor said my baby was fully developed and I was ready to safely deliver. Everything was positive: the baby was very healthy—good strong heartbeat, good movement. I stopped taking my medications and prepared for labor.

After waiting about thirty-six hours, I realized that I was no longer feeling any movement of my baby. This can be normal, but I decided to go into the clinic and be checked. When the doctor was unable to hear a heartbeat, my husband and I were sent to the hospital for an ultrasound to confirm "fetal demise."

Thus began the first of many strange questions that came to me while going through this experience.

Why don't we just use the words "dead" or" died"? We use many ways to discuss death without ever using the words dead or died. We are "sorry for the loss," the person "expired," "at the time of his passing," "eternal rest," "departure from this world," "cessation of life"—anything to soften the impact of death. In our culture, with widespread access to quality medical treatment, we often view death as outside of the natural cycles. Babies are a symbol of life, a sign that the cycle of life is continuing in its normal pattern. When a baby dies, all those perceived natural cycles are destroyed and those involved need to re-explore what they believe about natural cycles.

After the death of my baby was confirmed by ultrasound, we were given an appointment to meet with our doctor at 1:00 p.m. (two hours later) to discuss our options.

What kinds of options are there when your baby has died? How could there possibly be options? Our baby had died! I called my mom from the ultrasound room and told her that the baby had died. We arranged to meet at my house to wait the two hours for my appointment.

I arrived home to chaos. My mom had arrived earlier and spread the news. My grandmother, who had been caring for my fifteen-month-old son, was distraught. Everyone was moving around constantly, grieving loudly and not sure what to do. As for me, I remember being very focused. I wanted to hold my baby. I calmly got together what I needed to take to the hospital, while my husband called people to tell them the news. I remember when he told his mom that we had "lost the baby," my grandmother muttered, "That baby is not lost. We know where it is." I asked my mom if she wanted to come to the hospital to hold the baby after I delivered. It caught her by complete surprise, but she agreed to come.

At the doctor's office, I found that my "options" involved whether I wanted to be induced for labor or return home to wait for labor to begin on its own. But I wanted to hold my baby! I opted to have labor induced. By 2:00 p.m. I was at the hospital with medications ready to start. By 5:10 p.m., Daniel Clarence was born—well, sort of.

Did you know that when a baby is stillborn you do not receive a birth certificate, only a death certificate? Does that mean that Daniel was never born?

My husband and I spent about three hours holding our baby. We shared this time with our mothers, my brother and sister-in-law, my father, and our pastor. Looking back, it was a blessed time. But living it was so painful. Pain darkened every picture. Everything was over, ended, final, before it had even begun!

That is what is so different about the loss of a baby. When someone has lived with us, we have memories to share, good times to laugh about, perhaps even tough times for which to forgive one another. We sense that the one dying needs to be celebrated for having lived and for who he or she had become.

However, when a baby is stillborn, what memories do you have? Do you share the good and bad times of the pregnancy? Do you keep reliving the labor and delivery? You have no memories from a lifetime of living to sustain you. You have only the bleakest of a future staring at you, and suddenly there seems to be no future worth living.

At our memorial service for Daniel, our pastor gave us a Bible verse from the book of Daniel: "As for you, go your way till the end. You will rest, and then, at the end of the days, you will rise to receive your allotted inheritance" (Daniel 12:13). Our pastor told us that our son Daniel had completed his purpose on this earth, and he did it without ever taking a breath.

In the short time that Daniel was with us—yes, without his even taking a breath—Daniel's death started us on a journey that has created growth and life. It is a journey that has been long and hard. At times I would have chucked it all just to have Daniel alive and part of our life. Children, and the experiences shared with them, change every parent. Now, more than thirteen years later, I can see that Daniel has changed me even more than my two living children have, and I wouldn't exchange the experience of being who I am today because of his death for the experience of raising Daniel.

What can I do to make this pain go away? I could not avoid it or go around it, go under it or go over it. The only way was to journey *through* it.

Grief is a natural part of life that very few of us will avoid. When I was in the midst of grief myself, or was supporting a loved one in grief, I treated it like a problem to be solved or a hardship that needed to be overcome. Then I found that facing grief directly, choosing to grieve and giving myself permission and time to experience grief, was my most direct route through the grief. If I tried to avoid my grief, I would find it waiting for me somewhere down the road.

How do I get through this grief? Before Daniel's death, I was heading down a road on my journey through life that seemed well planned and smooth. Then suddenly I was forced to take a turn that changed the direction of my life and my final destination. Now the road was new and unfamiliar.

Many times on this new road it seemed that the old road was "just right over there." When new to grief, I exerted a lot of energy trying to get back to the old road, where life was good and the future secure. Now, as a veteran of grief, I can tell you that the old road was simply a mirage. My efforts to return to it wasted energy that I could have put to better use elsewhere.

I spent approximately three years after Daniel's death just trying to keep my head above water. Two months after Daniel died, my mother had told me that she was so proud of the way that I was handling Daniel's death. Because I needed her to be proud of me, I made sure that I "handled" it. In reality, I stuffed all my grieving down deep inside myself.

As my grieving process continued, however, I learned that grief couldn't be stuffed forever. It needed to get out and be experienced.

I hadn't allowed it to flow as grief, so it found its way out however it could.

For me, my grief came out as anger. I was mad at everyone and everything.

> I was mad at Daniel
> for dying.
> I was mad at myself
> for being mad at my child.
> I was mad at my husband
> because he didn't understand.
> I was mad at my children
> because they were children.
> I was mad at God
> for choosing to take Daniel.
> I was mad, mad, mad!

Eventually I realized that I could not continue to live this way, stuck on the new road but always wanting the old road back. I approached Marty McNunn at my church and asked her to counsel with me. She led me through a series of sessions that enabled me to recognize how so many of my feelings were flowing out of my grief over the loss of Daniel. She then helped me to let go of Daniel and to quit trying to get back on the old road. I started a healthier journey down the new road and, in the thirteen years since Daniel died, I have often received affirmation that the new road offers opportunities that could not have been a part of my life before.

Why? What was the purpose of Daniel's death? The "why" of Daniel's death was a huge obstacle to me in the beginning of my grief. I have heard many other women express the same need to understand why.

What I have learned over the years is that the "why?" isn't as big as it once was.

> Would understanding *why*
> have diminished the sorrow I felt?
> Would understanding *why*
> have filled my empty arms?
> Would understanding *why*
> have given me trust in the journey
> down this new road?

It is easy to think that knowing why would have solved many of the stumbling blocks on the journey through grief, but "why?" is not usually a question that is answered to our satisfaction.

Over time, I found that I began to experience healing when I began to create purpose in the midst of my grief. My purpose came from using what I had gone through to help other moms traverse their loss, and from using the ache in my soul to reach out in tenderness to those around me who were also aching. Then I finally found a satisfactory answer to the haunting question of "why?"

"He comforts us in all our troubles so that we can comfort others. When others are troubled, we will be able to give them the same comfort God has given us" (2 Corinthians 1:4). I have been comforted in my grief. I hold out to other grieving mothers that same hope of comfort in the years to come.

Are you a mother whose baby has died? I would encourage you to share your story of grief with someone else who is grieving. By sharing your story, I believe you will receive comfort yourself, just as I have and continue to do even today.

My Precious Child

In memory of my son

Life without you isn't the same.
Others seem to forget your name.
The pain at times is so real, so intense.
You're my child,
and will always be.
Your light will shine
if only through me.
Life goes on—although you're gone.
Old friends are different—and new ones help Mommy move on.
I wish everyone could see
the you who lives on in me.
You are my child, and will always be.
Your light will shine if only through me.

—Kathy Evans

Other Significant
Deaths

One of Our Parts
Is Missing

———

KARRIE HAMILTON and KEN LINDE, Coworkers

Scripture speaks of many parts making up one body and emphasizes that not all the parts are the same. This analogy is also true of a business organization. Our midsized printing company is one "body" composed of many different people, each making his or her own unique and valuable contribution. It is sometimes difficult not to assume that every part will be in place doing its thing for the good of the whole. This notion came crashing down for us one August day when our preproduction manager was involved in a fatal motorcycle accident.

We were reminded over and over that we must never take anyone or anything for granted. Our company had come to rely on Todd's printing knowledge and skill for nearly twenty-five years. He was a valuable resource to every element of the company. His death would cause work-related repercussions for our employees and customers alike. Everyone in the company attended the funeral, and we hosted a "Tribute to Todd Day" for employees, customers, family, and friends. Everyone felt lifted up and supported during these emotion-filled days.

In the days after the ceremonies and tributes, we realized that we had not only lost a valuable employee, we had also lost a friend and mentor. Todd's absence underscored the depth of his importance to us. Todd had a profound love and appreciation for those people he worked with, especially those directly in his care. He possessed a "can do" attitude even when workload and deadlines loomed large before us. He brightened the workplace with his smile, laughter, and affirmative manner.

Each person in the company had to deal with losing Todd, and it became clear that there would be a sustained period of grieving that would affect each person differently. It would also affect us as a group. We had worked together. We had relied on each other. We had trusted that each workday, we would all be at our stations, ready to do the tasks set before us. In some ways, our relationship was as strong as many family relationships, and we relied on our coworkers for our individual successes. Although not related by blood or marriage, we were all part of that one body, and we felt as though part of it had been ripped away.

As we have processed our loss over these past months, we have taken the steps to fill Todd's position in the company, all the while aware that we will never truly replace him. We did name our conference area in honor of Todd. It has been said that Todd's vibrant spirit remains, but yet we feel an emptiness.

Yes, no one or anything will ever replace Todd, and we encounter daily reminders of his absence. While we'll go on and continue doing great printing for our customers, it just doesn't feel the same. One of our parts is missing.

Grandma— A Constant in My Life

LISA HICKS

From my birth to age forty-one, when Grandma died, she was an incredible woman in my life.

I loved her with all my heart.

I have wonderful memories. I spent many nights in my childhood years at Grandma's.

I will never forget those mornings at her house when I'd lie down on the bed and raise my feet to her chest while she put my socks on. Why is that such a vivid memory? I don't know. Maybe because she always made me feel so loved and secure. I was very crabby when I'd have to leave to go home, without understanding why. I just didn't want to leave Grandma's. She spoiled me!

Grandma took me on my first airplane ride at age ten. We went to visit her sister in San Jose, California. Also, Grandma made the world's best chocolate chip cookies. I think most children in St. Paul Park, Minnesota, knew of Grandma's cookies.

Some of my favorite memories are of Christmas Eve at Grandma's home. Her house was very small, but all fifteen of us managed to somehow fit in that tiny living room full of Christmas presents, even if some of us had to sit on the stairs! On my twenty-first birthday, Grandma was there, along with my parents and my paternal grandparents. I remember so well another flight with Grandma, to visit her sister in Reno, Nevada.

Then there were all the day-to-day visits, when we saw movies together, walked hand in hand shopping, played bingo together, always with those wonderful chocolate chip cookies just waiting for me to pluck them from the jar.

Yes, Grandma was always a big part of my life. If I wasn't visiting her and Grandpa on Portland Avenue in St. Paul Park, I was often on the phone talking with her.

One of the hardest things she ever did was to move out of her home of sixty years and into a wonderful senior apartment building in Hastings, Minnesota. I helped her move and sell her home. I was elated because she was so close to my home, and I could spend nearly every day with her.

At age eighty-six, Grandma was still young. She was always on the go, never staying seated for long. She loved life, and loved her family and friends! Then one day Grandma called to tell me she was not feeling well. I immediately went to her apartment and took her to the hospital. Later that evening, I took her back home. "If you don't feel well," I told her, "call me no matter what time of the night it is: I will be there for you."

The next morning when I called her, there was no answer. Mother had called Grandma, too, with no response. I knew then that Grandma had died. There was no doubt in my mind. I wailed and wailed. My husband said, "You don't know anything yet. She could be in the lobby talking with the ladies." No. I knew she was not. I knew it in my heart. There was emptiness.

As soon as we could, we met my parents and we went together to Grandma's apartment. We found her there, "sleeping" in her bed. She was holding her rosary in her hand like she did every night. She looked very peaceful. She died in her sleep, just the way she always wanted to go. Now she is with Grandpa and their son, my uncle Gene.

The next three months after her death I was in a fog. I cried at home; I cried at work. I did not feel like talking much with my friends or my family.

I didn't feel like doing anything. I have always been a very active person. But now I would come home from work and fall on the couch or on the bed. I wouldn't even turn on the television. If my daughter would let me, I would just lie there and fall asleep. I would even fall asleep at work.

I was doing the motions, but not really living. Now I know what depression was. Then, however, I did not realize I was going into depression. I just knew that it was not fun and I wanted out.

When my husband told me that I needed help, I knew he was right. I began seeing a counselor to talk over my feelings and explain what the depression was doing to my life. I spoke with my mother about it and realized that she too was in depression and needed help. Together we decided to go to a grief group.

We discovered that the grief group was a place to talk about our mourning. It was also a place to listen to other people's experiences. We started to realize that we were not alone. What we were feeling, others might be feeling, too. We also learned that mourning is a process one needs to go through, and there is no particular length of time before it ends—that is different for everyone.

I know now that, if you are grieving, the feelings you are experiencing are normal. You are not alone. Do things to pamper yourself: take a candlelit bath; get a manicure; find a new hobby or interest; go to a movie or to the theater. Don't give up on life. Continue to talk about and remember your loved one. Make a scrapbook about your loved one. Keep those memories alive. Continue to laugh and love—just as my grandma always did.

Yes, I miss Grandma so much. After five months, I still feel as if she's here, and I feel the need to pick up the phone and call her. She should be here; she was never supposed to leave me. She was full of life and she had so much love to give.

I do believe that Grandma is still with me, watching over me, and that I can talk with her at any time. Recently, I visited her grave and asked her to help me apologize to a friend whom I had hurt during this process. When I got home from visiting Grandma's grave, that friend I hadn't talked to for months called me on the telephone as soon as I walked in the door.

Thank you again, Grandma. You were always there for me, and you still are!

Be merciful to me, O Lord, for I am in distress; my eyes grow weak
with sorrow, my soul and my body with grief.
My life is consumed by anguish and my years by groaning;
my strength fails because of my affliction,
And, my body grows weak.
But, I trust in you, O Lord; I say, "You are my God."
My times are in your hands.

—Psalm 31: 9–10, 14 (NIV)

Loss upon Loss

MARTY McNUNN

I had no idea when I began putting together this manuscript that I would soon experience my own personal grief. While one would think that my training and knowledge of how to grieve for a significant loss would make it easier for me, all of that just escaped me. While I knew in my head what I needed to do, my heart was not responding. I could give good advice to my family, but I had to talk myself into doing the grief work that I knew, on a head level, at least, would help me.

In this past year, I have had three significant family members die. Each death compounded the grief I'd felt for the others.

On New Year's Eve 2004, I received a phone call that a favorite uncle had died. I knew he had been ill and had planned to attend his funeral, but I was on a winter getaway in Florida and he lived in Washington State. It was impossible to get there in time. My heart hurt because I so wanted to be there, and for days I felt deep sadness and disappointment.

A few months later we learned that something was wrong with my granddaughter Andrea's baby, due in September. After many tests we were told the baby (a girl) suffered from Trisomy 18 (a chromosome disorder that causes birth defects). Her chances for life were slim.

On July 16, 2005, two months before her due date, my great-granddaughter Elora Grace was born—and died. Her death was the most significant loss I have experienced since the death of my parents many years ago. My heart ached for the baby's mother (my granddaughter Andrea) and her loss.

I can still remember the spiritual connection with the baby, Elora Grace, that came over me when I held that three-and-a-half pound, precious little baby. Even today, months later, I can close my eyes and feel her in my arms. I am so happy I had the chance to hold her.

My family and I walked in a fog of numbness for weeks. Sadness over the loss of our dreams for Elora Grace was overwhelming. Through this difficult time, the strength of our family ties grew even greater, and we all supported each other. When one was having a bad day, another would be okay, so we became a support system for each other.

I am thankful for my faith in God. I can't imagine going through such a hurtful event without this faith. Even though my heart hurt and sadness hung heavy upon me, I knew that the Lord was with me, strengthening and comforting me. He gave the assurance that Elora Grace was secure in His arms and that I would see her again one day.

Just weeks after Elora Grace's death, another significant uncle died. He had lived with my family during his college years and was like a brother to me. There again, I was so disappointed because I couldn't attend his funeral. His death brought back my grief from Elora's death. Sometimes the tears were so intense I felt I couldn't breathe. For a number of weeks, I suffered extreme fatigue and lack of motivation. It was easier to sit and do nothing than use the energy to get up and out. Having a job to go to was helpful but tiring. Most days I came home and fell asleep, sometimes sleeping for hours.

As I had seen happen so often for other grieving people, now the Hastings grief group became my support system and helped me through my personal loss. I truly became one of the grieving as we worked together to come to a better place with our grief.

One truth we discovered is that time alone doesn't heal, but it is like a friend, helping by just being there. I have also learned that, while grief itself is not easy, living with grief does get easier. As I have been reminded too often lately, it hurts when we lose a significant loved one, but I've also learned that we must move on. Educating ourselves and building a strong support system helps very much. It is in recognizing physical and emotional symptoms and knowing what to do about them that we gain the power to overcome.

Unthinkable

JOHN STROHSCHEIN, Pastor
Hope Lutheran Church, Hastings, Minnesota

"On Saturday, Oct. 8, 2005, gunshots rang out on Hastings' Vermillion Street, sending shock waves throughout the community after the murders of Peter and Patricia Niedere at their place of business." *(Hastings Star Gazette)*

Pete and Patty Niedere were members of Hope Lutheran Church. As their pastor, I was one of the first to be called that dreadful Saturday afternoon. I remember struggling to comprehend what had happened. Could this be a dream? I hoped to wake up and find all that pain gone, and that I could forget what I was seeing and hearing. It was so senseless, so sad and tragic. Two kind, generous, loving, Christ-like people had been shot to death—how unthinkable! That Saturday, October 8, 2005, is now and always will be indelibly scribed on my mind, heart, and soul. I will never be the same.

As time crept by that afternoon, I remember sitting with Dan (Pete and Patty's oldest son) on the Vermillion Street curb in front of their business, with police and media everywhere. It felt like a movie playing out before me, as my mind shouted, "Not Pete, not Patty, not in Hastings on the busiest street in town in broad daylight. How did anyone think they could get away with this violence?"

Then the unthinkable became even more so, as authorities announced that they had arrested seventeen-year-old Matthew Niedere, the couple's son. A criminal complaint charged Matthew and two of his schoolmates with planning the murders for Friday evening. When that plan did not work out, the complaint stated that Matthew and one schoolmate murdered the Niederes at their place of business.

I was faced with another level of tragedy, as an impossibly greater level of pain pounded my senses. Now the perpetrator of this terrible crime was no longer a nameless, evil person whom I so wanted to hate for doing this terrible thing. Now it was someone close to me, someone I knew. Yes, Matt—I had followed his hockey career—was like family to me. "Not Matthew, no way; not his mom and dad. Why, why?" repeated endlessly in my head as I struggled to understand. Why would he do such a horrendous thing? What was he thinking?

Throughout the long night, I felt as if I had lost all sense of reality, that everything seemed wrong. Nothing would ever be the same again for the Niedere family, for me personally, for our church, or for the city of Hastings; the weight of such knowledge was truly crushing.

I gradually came to understand that I would have to purposely change my thinking from hating an evil person to hating an evil act that person did but loving him nevertheless. I did not, and may never, understand Matt's actions, but I knew I must *choose* to love him as I had always known him to be: a loving, talented, happy teenager with so much to live for. My unconditional love for Matt was what the Lord, and also Pete and Patty, would expect of me, and I trusted the Lord to make it possible for me to separate Matt's deed from the person I knew him to be.

The sermon I had prepared for Sunday morning was based

on Philippians 4, verses 5, 8, and 9. In this passage, Paul told his church community that, regardless of what has happened, even with so many burdens, they could trust the Lord to provide faith, hope, and endurance to help them get through. Certainly, in our situation, we knew that without faith there would be no hope.

To provide in-depth help that was so crucial to everyone who had been touched by this tragedy, I made arrangements for professional counselors to come and spend two full days with anyone who needed their services. Many people joined us. We knew the Christian community was praying for us individually and as a church family, as we received cards and e-mails of condolences with prayers from all parts of our nation. Those prayers gave us the strength to keep on moving forward.

The funeral service itself became a heart-warming ecumenical effort. As St. Elizabeth Ann Seaton Catholic Church has the largest accommodations in town, they graciously made their facility available. About 3,000 people attended the visitation on Thursday evening, and more than 1,200 attended the memorial service the next day. Christians in Hastings became one body. The song "They Will Know We Are Christians by Our Love" was a reality. Anyone who knew Pete and Patty knew them for their loving and kind spirits.

People in the community felt compelled to demonstrate their love for Pete and Patty in a visible way. Many provided food or sent flowers. At the cemetery, planes performed a flyover: one was Pete's own plane piloted by a close friend. The others were from Pete's flying club. The planes flew over together, and then separated, with Pete's plane flying off alone. It was a very moving experience. Patty's golfing club honored her with a separate memorial service. The local cable TV station did an "Unsung Hero Tribute" for them. Yes, Pete and Patty are much loved in the community of Hastings.

As time has passed, we understand that some questions may

never be answered, but we are moving forward. The Hope congregation focused on Dan Niedere and his wife Angie. We became a loving support system for them, providing meals and helping them move into a new home. Although we will always miss Pete's and Patty's leadership, other church members have picked up the church responsibilities they formerly shouldered, enabling us to continue moving forward.

Now, several months later, we are seeing how good has started to come from this horrendous tragedy:

- The Hastings Christian community came together as one: regardless of beliefs or church affiliation, people interacted and worked together for the betterment of our community, and several pastors and their congregations prayed for and supported us.
- People have become more compassionate and giving.
- We have gained an understanding that not one of us is exempt from grief and pain, and that others will step in to help us when we also experience grieving and hurting.
- The community generously provided for financial needs, as people followed the example Pete and Patty had always demonstrated with their generous hearts.
- The media saw believers trusting and being Christ-like as they struggled to come to grips with an act that was so far from Christ-like; they saw that these believers never lost faith and hope, but trusted the Lord for strength and comfort.

Yes, God is still God. He has not left us, and He stands faithful with us in all situations. We strive to do what we know the Lord would want of us, and what Pete and Patty would want of us: to move on, and to love and support each other, and to live as Christ would want us to live.

Our faith in Jesus Christ gives us the assurance that Pete and Patty are together rejoicing in heaven and that we will see them again one day. For now and always on this earth, however, we miss them.

Rejoice! Let your gentleness be evident to all. The Lord is near.
Do not be anxious about anything, but in everything, by prayer and
petition, with thanksgiving, present your request to God.
And the peace of God, which transcends all understanding, will
guard your hearts and your minds in Christ.
Finally, whatever is true, whatever is noble, whatever is right, and
whatever is admirable—if anything is excellent or praiseworthy—
think on such things. Whatever you have learned or received or heard
from me, or seen in me—put it into practice.
And the God of peace will be with you.

—Philippians 4:5–9 (NIV)

Victims of Hurricane Katrina

FLORENCE FOX

My sister Bobbye and her husband, Frank, both aged seventy-six, were victims of Hurricane Katrina. They lived in Slidell, Louisiana, and received a direct hit on August 29, 2005. They lost everything they had in the hurricane: their home, their car, and all their possessions, except for one suitcase each.

Bobbye had been in poor health for the past few years, and she was not able to evacuate when the notice was given. Her family doctor had her admitted to the Slidell hospital. Frank evacuated with their son and his family to an area in central Mississippi. Shortly after, the hospital in Slidell was evacuated to a hospital in Meridian, Mississippi. After the hurricane, Bobbye was again transferred back to the Slidell hospital. It was then determined that she needed surgery on her back, but the hospital in Slidell was not equipped to handle it and she was transferred again to a hospital in Lacombe, Louisiana, where they performed the surgery.

On September 15, Bobbye and Frank, along with their dog, Monty, were sent by air ambulance to central Texas near Austin. Bobbye was admitted to Sagebrook Health Center, and Frank moved in with me. At first Bobbye did well at the nursing home, but gradually her health problems and the realization that she no longer had a home took its toll; she passed away on November 11, 2005.

The past few years Frank had been her principal caregiver. I know Frank is grieving for Bobbye and misses her, but he knows that her quality of life was gone and he is grateful that she is no longer living in pain. However, along with those feelings, there is a certain amount of guilt. He is no longer tied down to an invalid wife, and he is free to do some things he wants to do.

I have seen him several times with tears in his eyes as he watches the news coverage of New Orleans and Slidell in the aftermath of the hurricane. There are so many heart-wrenching stories of families like Frank and Bobbye who have lost everything and have no flood insurance to cover their losses and rebuild their homes.

My personal grieving for Bobbye is similar to Frank's. She was in so much pain and had so many health problems it was hard to be encouraged about her future. I am just grateful that God took her and I pray she is with Him. She was a believer, and I hold on to the promise that whoever believes in Jesus will be saved.

Death by Suicide

Why, Dad?

ANGIE McGINNIS

On June 6, 1999, my father, Bill, took his life. Three years to the day later, on June 6, 2002, I gave birth to my daughter, Gracie. I believe that God intentionally turned the anniversary of a day formerly full of grief into a day full of rejoicing.

In the meantime, though, it had been a difficult journey. Losing my father to suicide was so painful that all of us in the family—including my mother and my three brothers—didn't know how we were going to see our way through it. In our devastation, all we could do was to keep on loving one another, and talking and crying together, which we sometimes do even now, years later.

What amazes us is that, although my father's pain must have been so deep, those of us closest to him didn't recognize it. In fact, when I heard that he was dead, I thought for certain it was from a heart attack. None of us would ever have imagined that my father could choose to end his life. To know my dad was to know a man who was determined and hardworking, intelligent and family-orientated, successful and loving, a man with a strong sense of humor. He laid the foundation for our family's closeness and taught us wonderful values.

That fateful Sunday evening started as so many others had,

with our family sharing a cookout, and my dad joking around. Later, though, I noticed a different look about him. "I'm not sticking around much longer, so you don't have to worry," he stated. When he wouldn't explain what he meant, I got frustrated and left. It was the only time I can remember leaving my dad without a hug, a kiss, and an "I love you."

If only I had known that was the last conversation I would ever have with him!

Later, after learning of my dad's death, the family gathered again. "What are we going to tell people?" my mother asked. "We are going to tell people the truth," my brother Jeff replied. I believe God gave us that insight, and it formed the basis for the eulogy I delivered at my dad's funeral. "I will honor my dad by the way I choose to lead my life from this day forward," I said.

That is not to say that I could bypass the work of my own grieving. Sometimes that meant tears, other times anger, confusion, or hurt; sometimes it meant finding joy in a happy memory. I found it helpful to spend time with friends, and to attend a grief group. Other times I spoke with a counselor, or read, or wrote in my journal. Like someone on a roller coaster ride, I hit lots of highs and lows.

People often commented that "time will heal." That may appear to be the case, but I believe that, in reality, it's not the passing of time itself that heals. I healed because of the work of grieving I did as time passed.

Throughout this time, I kept trying to understand what had happened to my dad, and began to educate myself about depression and suicide. Later this study became the new focus of my graduate thesis. I also began speaking to groups about depression and suicide. At one point, a young high school student at a critical juncture in her life sought out lifesaving help after listening to my presentation to her class.

I once questioned where God was in all of this. Now I can

thank God that His grace and mercy allow me to bring something positive from this gut-wrenching experience.

Six years after my dad's suicide, I feel that I am honoring my father by working through my grief and finding ways to assist others who struggle with the same issues. Hopefully I can help these grieving souls catch a glimpse of the other side of their pain, where hope, love, laughter, and peace still exist.

"I miss you, Dad . . ."

Kevin

EUGENIE (GENE) HARPER

My son, Kevin, was thirty-one years old when he took his own life. Even today, after six years, it is difficult to talk about this terrible loss.

So many times, I've looked back over Kevin's life and tried to understand why this happened. It's true that, as a small child, Kevin was moody and withdrawn, and he was not an easy child to rear. A defiant child, he refused to do anything asked of him. He didn't like school and usually refused to do his schoolwork. Then, in his early teens, he began to experiment with drugs.

Kevin made his first attempt at suicide when he was a teenager. For the first time in many years, he had spent the summer with his dad, from whom I was divorced. A few days after Kevin returned, he overdosed. He was admitted to a treatment center, where he stayed until he was nineteen years old.

Kevin met a young woman at the center, and they got married. Although he remained drug-free for about two years following the birth of his son, Kevin and his wife divorced and she moved out of state, taking the child with her. Kevin left town, too. He didn't tell me where he was going, and I had no contact with him for two and a half years.

By this time, I had remarried, and my husband felt we needed to find Kevin. We finally located him in a halfway house in northern Minnesota. He had changed so much I hardly recognized him: my 130-pound son now weighed at least 200 pounds. For the next fifteen years, on prescription drugs for depression, Kevin was in and out of treatment centers and halfway houses. Then he began mixing street drugs with his prescription medications, and added alcohol and gambling to his addictive lifestyle.

During those fifteen years, Kevin threatened suicide a number of times, but always called 911 when he would become scared. Still, no one seemed to take his threats seriously, because too many times he'd used them just to find a nice place where he could live and be taken care of. Nevertheless, I would suggest that if you have a family member or friend who talks about suicide or attempts to take his or her life, you should not take it lightly. Get help immediately.

Eventually, Kevin began seeing a mental health counselor regularly. After a few years, his medication was regulated and Kevin could hold down a job and live on his own. His life seemed stable. However, in June of 1999, he once again attempted suicide—successfully, this time. He died alone in his apartment. No note was found. Friends speculated that he was distressed because he had lost his paycheck gambling and had no money for his son's upcoming visit.

I spent the next few months in a fog. I couldn't believe this had happened, and I blamed myself for not keeping in closer contact with Kevin. I soon began to experience multiple health problems: heart, stomach, emotional distress, and such extreme fatigue I couldn't even take a shower without help. It wasn't until I attended the grief group in November 2000 that I realized my health problems were probably from grief. I wasn't alone; others in the group reported similar problems associated with their grief.

Eventually, the group became a secure and safe place for me

to talk and cry, to ask questions, and to work through my grief in a healthy way. I am so thankful I had a place to go where others knew what I was experiencing, where others had a loved one who had taken his or her own life. Remarkably, no one blamed me for Kevin's choice. I learned that I really wasn't going crazy, and that the pain wouldn't always be so incredibly unbearable.

My Only Child

PATTY DOFFING

A week after his high school graduation, my son, Matt, kissed and hugged me before leaving for work. "I love you, Mom," he said. I let him take the truck because he and some friends were planning to attend a couple of parties after work that evening. When he didn't come home that night, I borrowed my mom's car to get to work. During the day, I called his cell phone a number of times. But he still hadn't come home or called when I got home from work, and I was worried. Matt always told me where he was going and always answered his phone.

Later that day the sheriff called and said that my unoccupied truck had been found in a ditch south of town. Worry reached a peak now, as Matt's friends joined my search for him.

Arriving at the site where my truck had been found, I knew right away something bad had happened. One of Matt's friends ran to me and hugged me. "I'm so sorry, I'm so sorry," he kept repeating. Then the sheriff told me that three of my son's friends had found Matt. He was hanging from a tree limb, down a ravine near the place where the truck went off the road. They were bringing up his body right at that time.

My whole world went into a slow-moving spin. Nothing

seemed right. I knew people were talking, but I couldn't hear them, because of my own screams: "NO, NO, NO, NO!"

When I was allowed to see his body, I remember how cold he was. But I couldn't grasp the truth. All the way to the hospital I kept thinking, "Matt's going to wake up as soon as he gets warm. He'll be there waiting for me."

Of course that didn't happen. Instead, I collected Matt's belongings. My mom had come to the hospital, and we drove home in a daze. There we found the yard full of Matt's friends, and we pieced together what had happened the night before. Matt and two friends left the party early Thursday morning. Matt was driving drunk, they said, missed a curve, and went off in a ditch, where the truck stuck between two trees. They decided to walk back to the party to get help, but Matt told his friends, "I can't go any farther, come back and get me." They left him sitting along the side of the road. It was the last time anyone would see him alive.

Through the difficult days ahead, I still struggled to believe that Matt was really dead and I would never again see him, never hug him, never hear him say, "I love you, Mom."

On the day of Matt's funeral, the church was full of teenagers. Even his kindergarten teacher and his former babysitter attended, and some businesses closed for the day. The funeral director estimated that 1,600 people attended.

The days and nights following Matt's funeral are just a blur in my mind. I couldn't sleep, seldom went out, forgot to eat, and was rapidly losing weight. Lonely, I missed him so much my heart actually hurt. "He was my only child; he was all I had!" I found myself waiting for him to come in the door, and sometimes I tried to believe that he was just on vacation.

Then, a friend sent me a brochure from the Hastings Area Grief Coalition. "Why don't you go, just once," she said. Although it took a lot of courage to get there the first time, I knew I needed help.

As soon as I walked in the door, I was welcomed with friendly faces and warm smiles. Then when I tried to talk, I couldn't do it without crying. But that didn't bother anyone; they just cried with me. It was so freeing to tell my story to these good listeners. They didn't pass judgment or assign guilt; they just accepted me for who I was: a grieving mother.

Once I started going to the grief group, I could hardly wait for the next week's meeting. Each week gave me strength to continue on for seven more days. Over the next couple of years, I learned what grief does to a person, physically, emotionally and spiritually. I learned to deal with life one day at a time. Even when I lost my job, I could put into practice the coping skills I heard from the educational speakers.

Oh, yes, I still occasionally have down days. However, I don't have the same heaviness of grief anymore that drove my life for years. Now I try to stay positive and to have a good outlook, and I once again have hope for my future. For a short time, I had the privilege to serve as a facilitator for the grief group, and found it rewarding to help others work through their grief.

At the present time I am training to become a licensed practical nurse. That helps gives purpose to my days. Yes, I have learned to live with my grief, but there will always be a hole in my life. Still, I believe that Matt is cheering me on and is proud of my accomplishments. That keeps me going.

I Had to Learn
the Hard Way

ANONYMOUS

The day I was told my daughter took her own life, I felt like I died, too. The pain was beyond my ability to a handle. I was so sad. I felt guilty and so sorry for not being there for her. It felt like my heart had literally broken. The first few weeks after her death are a blank to me. All I remember is sitting in a chair, with people coming and going, and thinking, "My child is dead, life is trivial."

The only way I felt I could survive was to numb the pain, and I began to drink daily. I would go to work and drink until I passed out, day after day. I felt nothing, did nothing, and cared about nothing. As long as I didn't have to think or feel, I thought I could manage.

Finally, a friend challenged me to get some help, if not for myself, then for my other children. I joined Alcoholics Anonymous and began to attend the daily meetings and to work the 12 Step Program for Recovery. After a few days of sobriety, I realized I had to deal with my grief. All that alcohol and drugs had only delayed the process.

It was suggested I attend a grief support group. The education program was an invaluable tool for my recovery. Prior to my daughter's death no significant person in my family had died, so I had no idea what it felt like to grieve or what grief would do to my entire being.

The more I learned, the more I saw myself in the stories of others, and the more I could identify with their pain. The group was caring and compassionate, and everyone was a good listener. It became a safe and comfortable place for me.

I still hurt. I still regret not being there for my daughter when she needed me. I will never get over that. But I continue each day, one day at a time. I have remained sober with the help of the AA program.

Educational Information

Depression and Depressive Illnesses: Facts You Should Know

———

SAVE • Suicide Awareness Voices of Education™

What Are Depressive Illnesses?

Depressive illnesses are total-body illnesses that affect a person's thoughts, feelings, behavior, physical health, and appearance. They affect all areas of a person's life: home, school, work, and social.

These illnesses are different from the ordinary "blues," which are normal feelings that eventually pass. Depressive illnesses last for months or years with varying patterns.

People with depressive illnesses cannot talk themselves either into feeling good or out of feeling bad. They cannot snap themselves out of it. Many times, society assumes people suffering from depression are just lazy or lacking in motivation to get their lives together. People with depression are often labeled as having a behavior or attitude problem. This simply is not true.

Depressive illnesses are not due to personal weakness or a character flaw, but are biological illnesses related to imbalanced or disrupted brain chemistry. The brain is an organ of the body and can get "sick," just as the heart, liver, or kidneys can. People with depression and other depressive illnesses have a disease that requires diagnosis and treatment by a doctor.

What Causes a Depressive Illness?

Genetic, psychological, and environmental factors all play a role in how and when a depressive illness may manifest itself. Because these are illnesses, stressful life events do not have to be present, but they can trigger or exacerbate the depression. Depression can arise at a time when it would appear that there is no reason for a person to be depressed, because it can appear out of nowhere.

People of all ages, including infants and children who may be born with a chemical imbalance, can suffer from depressive illnesses. Since they may be genetic, a person who is predisposed may be at higher risk for developing depressive illnesses than those who do not have these illnesses in their family. This does not mean everyone will inherit a depressive illness. However, by recognizing the signs and symptoms of depressive illnesses, people can seek the treatment they need to avoid suffering for months or years.

How Is a Depressive Illness Diagnosed?

Depression is the most common, and most misdiagnosed, illness in America. Over 15 million Americans suffer from depressive illnesses in a given year. We are not ashamed of having any other biological illness, such as heart disease or diabetes, nor should we be ashamed of having a depressive illness. People seek treatment for many illnesses, just as people need to be willing to seek medical treatment for a depressive illness. It would not be expected that people treat their diabetes on their own; nor should it be expected that people treat their depression on their own.

To determine whether a depressive illness is present or not, a thorough medical examination is essential.

Many drugs used to treat other illnesses, such as cancer, heart disease, high blood pressure, or arthritis, as well as oral contraceptives and some antibiotics, can trigger depressive illnesses.

Long-term or sudden illnesses can also bring on or exacerbate a depressive illness. Neurological disorders, hormonal disorders, infections, and tumors can "mimic" the symptoms of depressive illnesses.

If all medical tests come out negative, or if chronic physical pain does not respond to treatment, there is a strong possibility that a depressive illness exists.

Signs and Symptoms of Depression in Adults

If a combination of several of the following symptoms occurs for a period of time (such as two weeks or more), the person may be suffering from a depressive illness. The individual needs to contact his or her health care provider for a thorough examination:

- Persistent sad or empty mood
- Feelings of hopelessness, helplessness, guilt, pessimism, or worthlessness
- Drug/alcohol abuse
- Change in appetite
- Chronic fatigue, or loss of interest in ordinary and once pleasurable activities
- Disturbances in eating or sleeping patterns
- Irritability, increased crying, anxiety, chronic worry or fear
- Apparent hypochondria (however, the sufferer actually feels symptoms; they are not imagined, yet there is no other medical explanation for them)
- Difficulty concentrating, remembering, or making decisions
- Thoughts of suicide, suicide plans or attempts
- Persistent physical symptoms or pains that do not respond to treatment: headaches; stomach problems; pain in the back, neck, joints, and mouth

Can Depressive Illnesses Be Treated?

Yes! Depressive illnesses are highly treatable, in various ways, depending on the type and severity of the illness, and the age of the person being treated.

Warding off depressive illnesses means taking care of one's health through good exercise and eating habits. Stress management has proven to be helpful as well. Many people with these illnesses are treated through a combination of antidepressant medication and psychotherapy.

Antidepressant medications correct the chemical imbalance of the person's brain. They are not addictive drugs. If the person taking the antidepressant does not have depression, the drug will not have any effect on him. Antidepressants are not a mood-altering drug; they will not make a person happier or provide him with more energy. In simple terms, they regulate the chemicals in the brain that control our mood. Some people take antidepressants for a short period of time, while others take them for a lifetime. In either case, it is imperative that the sufferer seeks advice from a doctor who will prescribe the most effective treatment for the individual person's depressive illness.

Facts about Suicide

If depressive illnesses are left untreated, they can be fatal. Approximately 30,000 people in the U.S. kill themselves every year. Researchers suggest that this number could actually be three times higher than this, since many cases are inaccurately reported. Some are reported as accidents, rather than suicide, because of the stigma attached to suicide deaths.

The *Journal of the American Medical Association* has reported that 95 percent of all suicides occur at the peak of a depressive episode. The illness distorts persons' thinking, so that they do not think rationally. They may not even know they have a depressive illness that can be treated. The sufferers want to end their pain, and death is seemingly the only way to do this. Healthy people do not want to die. Unfortunately, the stigma attached to suicide deaths, more often than not, prevents the person from seeking treatment. Fortunately, the stigma is lifting as more and more education on depression and suicide takes place.

What Are the Danger Signs of Suicide?

- Statements about hopelessness, helplessness, or worth-lessness. For example: "Life is useless." "Everyone would be better off without me." "I won't be around much longer," etc.
- Self-destructive behavior, such as alcohol/drug abuse, self-injury, etc.
- Loss of interest in activities/things once cared about
- Talking or joking about suicide
- Statements about being reunited with a loved one
- Giving possessions away, making arrangements, setting affairs in order
- Unusual visiting or calling of people they care about; saying goodbye
- Preoccupation with death
- Suddenly happier and calmer (when suicide is planned out the sufferer feels less agitated and more at peace)
- Obsession with guns or knives

Just because the person is doing any of these things does not mean his mind is made up. He can be stopped! The person's pain is what he or she wants to end, not his or her life. The sufferer feels that there is no way out other than through death since he or she is not in a rational state of thinking.

What Should You Do If You Suspect Someone May Be Suicidal?

Ask that person! That may sound scary, or too simple, or ab-surd, but by asking him if he ever feels so badly that he would want to end his life, you may be opening the door to the help the individual is seeking. Remember: the sufferer wants to end his pain, and having someone recognize that he is hurting is often the first and most important step in seeking help for the individual.

Always take a suicide threat seriously and never keep it a secret. The threat is a cry for help that must not be minimized with comments suggesting that you don't believe they would do such a thing, or that they have everything to live for, or how hurt their family would be. These comments only increase the guilt and feelings of hopelessness that the person may be feeling.

When confronted, the person may respond angrily, defensively, or with denial. If he does, be persistent in expressing your concern. Talk openly about the symptoms and warning signs that are of concern to you. Suggest seeking medical attention and offer to go with him. Remember you could be saving a life by speaking openly and in a nonjudgmental manner to the person needing help. If he answers yes, get him to promise not to hurt himself, do not leave him alone, and seek medical help as soon as possible. This can be obtained from a local hospital, health care provider, or by calling a suicide crisis line such as 1-800-SUICIDE. Reassure the person that these feelings and thoughts are part of the disease of depression, that they are temporary, and that they can be treated. Suicide can be prevented with the right intervention and medical treatment.

Physical Reactions to Death and Grief

——

BARBARA JORENBY, BSN, RN, MA

Most grieving people are aware that the mixed-up emotional state of grieving leads to physical symptoms. Health care professionals and contemporary researchers also affirm the strong influence that strong emotions, such as grief, exert on physical functions.

Grief symptoms are part of our body's basic instinct for survival—the "fight or flight" response. When we are upset and stressed, our nervous system automatically produces chemicals called hormones, including adrenalin. This release of hormones causes the following feelings:

- breathlessness/frequent sighing
- Increased heart rate
- cold, clammy hands
- headache
- tightness in the chest
- heart palpitations
- dry mouth

As the stress of grief continues, our body tries to adapt by releasing other hormones, such as aldosterone, cortisol, and thyroxine, which can result in the following feelings:

- dizziness
- nausea
- change in appetite
- anxiety

We can take steps to help our body, but to try to stop the re-action would be similar to eating an apple and telling your stomach not to digest it. It won't work, because the process is beyond our conscious control. Since the body, mind, and soul are all intercon-nected, experiencing a trauma in any one of these areas will also affect the other areas.

Simple Reactions

Reactions to death will vary among people, and reaction to a sudden death will likely be different from the reaction to a death that had been anticipated. Following are some examples of symp-toms people have reported when they are grieving:

Digestive System:
- changes in appetite; digestion, and/or bowel elimination

Nervous System:
- anxiety
- vision problems
- trouble sleeping
- headaches
- restlessness, lack of concentration
- odd sensations, such as numbness

Heart and Circulation:
- rapid heart beat; irregular palpitations; and/or high blood pressure

Respiratory System:
- shortness of breath; inability to take a deep breath; and/or asthma attacks

Immune System:
- Lack of rest and/or inadequate nutrition lead to lowering of your immunities, which leaves you susceptible to colds or other infection.

While proper "self-care" is an important tool in helping your body, mind, and soul to recover, extreme problems may need medi-cation or therapy.

Here are some suggestions that will help you take better care of yourself:

- *Nutrition:* Eat a balanced meal, and stay on a regular meal schedule.
- *Sleep:* Get plenty of rest, and establish a regular bedtime routine.
- *Relaxation:* Make time for conscious periods of relaxation; use relaxation techniques such as meditation, prayer, and music.
- *Physical exercise:* Exercise releases endorphins, the "feel-good chemicals"; walk, run, or join a gym. Establish a regular exercise routine.
- *Communication with others:*
  Talk about your loved one and your grief feelings.
  Find a good friend with a listening ear.
  Join a grief support group.
  Talk to a clergy person.
- *Patience:* Be patient with yourself.

Grief is an individual process. While your experience is unique, you can be confident that other people have survived their unique grief walk, and that you will survive yours, too.

Grief and Chiropractic Care

―――

MELISSA MILLNER, DC, DACCP, FICPA

Chiropractic care is often overlooked as a vital part of helping your body through the grieving process. Numerous studies have show the amazing power chiropractic has to reduce stress and tension in your nervous system.

This not only decreases pain but also improves your immune function and emotional stability. Your nervous system includes your brain, spinal cord, and nerves, which carry all of the essential information to run every system of your body.

Without this vital information flow from the brain, your body simply can't work properly and you begin to lose your health physically and emotionally. When you have been through chemical, physical, and emotional stress, your nervous system is stressed as well, and it doesn't work as efficiently. With chiropractic care, your nerve flow will be restored, bringing back all the life your body needs to run properly and heal. You will begin to notice physical and emotional changes in your health as your body's communication system is restored.

Forgiving the Dead

RICHARD E. CLOSE, D.MIN, LICSW

It may seem odd to mention forgiveness as an essential part of grieving. After all, at a time like this, we are shattered at the loss of a dearly beloved person. We are probably in shock, just trying to take it in and get our minds to believe that what is happening is real. We are either consumed with emotions, or just plain numb. How, then, can anyone suggest to us that we should add something like forgiveness to the seemingly endless list of emotional mountains we are already climbing? Because you need to. Maybe not right way, but at some point, you need to. And the person you have lost needs you to as well.

Here are some of the reasons it may seem inappropriate or pointless to suggest that forgiving the dead is a necessary step to healing:

1. We are taught that it is important only to speak well of the dead.
2. As time passes, our sorrow and loneliness for the departed deepen. We tend to idealize them and forget that, just as they were wonderful, they also at times hurt us or failed us. These feelings are just as real, even if they are not "front and center" after our loved one has died.

3. It may seem "too late" once someone has died to do anything about reconciliation or to complete unfinished business with him or her.

4. To acknowledge that the departed one needs forgiveness
   might feel as if we are judging them negatively when they
   are no longer here to defend themselves. That can lead us
   to feel as if we are betraying their memory.

The truth is that, even when someone dies, we remain in relationship with him or her. How they treated us, well or ill, remains
alive and present with us. These things need attending to. Forgiving someone who has died brings completion and peace to the his-
tory you have had with your loved one. That completion can open
doors to an enduring, authentic connection with that person and
who they really were.

That is the best way to move forward while carrying their
presence in your heart and mind. To do this, we need to confront
the possibility that, mixed in with the love and yearning we still
feel, there may be leftover anger.

Here are some ways to admit this anger, acknowledge it, and
bring it into your continued connection to the one you have lost, even
as you build a life without him or her on a daily, physical basis:

1. Acknowledge that, by dying, your loved one has left
   you. Of course, you know that in most cases people
   do not want to die, but the fact remains that he or she,
   against your wishes, has left you alone to carry on. He
   or she did not have your permission to leave. As irrational as that might sound, that feeling is real and needs
   attention.

2. Recognize that, while your loved one is now in that place
   of peace, you are left to struggle on. Knowing he or she is
   in that place of peace may be comforting, and you would
   not wish anything less for the departed one, yet the fact

remains that your life has now doubled in difficulty without him or her by your side or in your life.

3. Remember that we generally get angry with people who
do not apologize or make amends for the hurtful or
thoughtless things they had done or said to us. That is a
normal response. When someone close to us dies, it is a
sure bet that, mixed in with all the loving things they did
or said, are some rough spots that never got smoothed
over. These remain with us, and need some process of
recognition and reconciliation.

Forgiveness is often misunderstood to mean that no matter
what was done to you, you are required to forget it and let it go.
This is too simple.

Forgiveness does not call for us to say that what was done to
us is okay. In reality, forgiveness is something you can reach even
if the other person never acknowledges or agrees that they were in
the wrong. In forgiveness you are liberating yourself from holding
on to hurt, anger, or resentment.

The normal approach to forgiveness is no longer possible once
someone has died. There can be:

- No face-to-face encounter
- No expression of anger, hurt, or sadness
- No chance to hear his or her side
- No forgiving and making up

Here are five steps toward forgiving someone who has died,
even when it appears to be too late:

1. Remember in detail the specific action or words that you
are holding on to.
2. Reassure yourself that this process of reaching forgiveness
is aimed at building a new, ongoing connection with your
loved one and is not idle criticism after the fact.

3. Talk with your deceased loved one in your mind, or with someone you trust, about how you wish he or she had spoken or acted differently. Even a letter written to that loved one can have a powerful effect on how you later think and feel toward that person.

4. Turn in your prayer life to God—who is with your loved one now—and ask that you find or be given the strength to let the offense go. Ask for God to touch you and your loved one in reconciliation. This can be done in reverse if you feel bad about something you did or said that remained unfinished and unforgiven before he or she died.

5. When you are ready, make a symbolic act to mark the completion of this process. You may especially offer some time, work, or money to a cause that was important to your loved one. You may go to a place he or she loved. The ways in which this can be done are too numerous to list; the important thing is to do something. Action is powerful.

It is also important to mention that these steps might not radically change your feelings. Be careful not to use feelings as the final criteria for deciding if something you needed to happen has happened. The process of forgiving, like most of grieving, will be complicated by numerous emotions and conflicting thoughts. What will finally bring you peace will be your efforts to accomplish forgiveness. You can forgive the dead, and you can feel forgiven by the one who has died, when you acknowledge that death is not the end of the relationship.

Four Expressions of Caring

———

PASTOR CARRIE TOKHEIM, Hastings, Minnesota
With CHAPLAIN JOHN CARLSON,
St. Joseph's Hospital, St. Paul, Minnesota

The four expressions of caring can be used when there is need for healing of relationships, as well as for "letting go," and for grief work before, during, and after dying and death. The words are also helpful in personal and group rituals of remembering.

1. **I'm sorry.** These words initiate a time to share thoughts and feelings in an open and honest manner. It's a time when it is possible to experience forgiveness and reconciliation, and when we can acknowledge that we are sorry for anything that may be bothering us about our relationship with another person, even if that person has died.

   Be kind to one another, tenderhearted, forgiving one another as God in Christ has forgiven you.
   Ephesians 4:32 (NLT)

2. **I love you.** Some very meaningful "I love you's" can be said after honest "I'm sorry's" have been expressed. Just as people really do like to hear the words "I love you" said out loud, it is helpful for you to say them to your loved one who has died. Think about some of the things you

love about that person. This expression is not something to take for granted.

3. **Thank you for the person you have been in my life.** This is a time to do some life review, looking at the good times and maybe even some of the not-so-good times. Express thankfulness for who the person has been in your life.

Give thanks in all circumstances;
for this is the will of God in Christ Jesus for you.
1 Thessalonians 5:18 (NIV)

4. **Goodbye. I'll be okay.** This may be the hardest step to take, but it is very important. In saying goodbye, one both gives and receives permission to let go. It is not that there won't be pain and grieving, but at some point letting yourself and the other know that you will be okay is important. You are doing what you need to do to grieve well. Goodbye is short for "God be by you." It is a blessing and a promise.

Romans 8 reminds us that, among other things, Christ Jesus is our intercessor. It may be helpful to think that your words reach through the gate of death and into the silence of remembering, and by the grace of God these words are returned to you to bring you comfort and God's peace. This ritual of remembering can be helpful on special occasions with family and friends, as you share your thoughts and feelings with others.

Spiritual Issues in Grief

———

PASTOR CARRIE TOKHEIM, Hastings, Minnesota

Grief affects all of us physically, emotionally, and spiritually. The grief process will invite you to reorganize your belief system, re-identify who God is, and define the nature of your relationship. Your belief system can help with issues of anger, blame and forgiveness, as well as give you a framework for using your quiet time. There are people who can help you as you ponder. Going to church is helpful to some, but very hard for others.

No feelings are inappropriate; it is important that you not ignore or stuff them.

In their grief, many people think about suicide, but they need to look at the other side: their life is important to other people.

Faith is dynamic and constant. Hold on to what is helpful as long as it is helpful and then, when a new idea forms, take it to be progress and move ahead.

You may think of the grief process as a "test of faith," but you do have all you need to pass with flying colors. The process is between you and God. Others can help, but no one can tell you what to believe. No one, including family, will be where you are.

You must work through your belief system. What do you believe and what questions do you have?

People are not very comfortable talking about issues of faith. Good friends may say hurtful things out of ignorance or just to say something. They mean no harm, so let it go in one ear and out the other. You may find their sympathy cards more helpful. Hold on to what is helpful to you.

Find someone with whom you can talk about issues of faith, where you can express your thoughts and feelings safely and confidently. Do not look for answers. Look for prayer support and encouragement.

As you deal with your personal issues of grief:

- Be honest and patient with yourself and God.
- Be open to new ways of thinking about life and death, as those ideas are helpful.
- Practice faith to the extent you can. Do what you can and push yourself a little.
- Plan rituals of remembering.

Loneliness

—

MARGE EATON HEEGAARD, MA, ATR, LICSW

"The loneliness that accompanies grief is an assault on the meaning of life itself" (Edgar Jackson in *The Many Faces of Grief*). It is a threat to the inner security system of an individual.

When a loved person is happy, that happiness is shared.

When your loved one is injured, you feel that injury.

When your loved one dies, you feel that impact also. You have invested part of yourself in the person you loved, and that part of you is gone. As a bereaved person, you grieve for that part of you that is lost, also.

Is this loneliness part of the self-grieving for its missing part? Is it something that can be resolved? If so, how?

You can get a positive answer to this question, but you are just as likely to refuse a positive answer. Instead, you may prefer to hold on to grief and to your willingness to suffer as a result of it, as proof of your love for the one who has died. But this can cripple life. While holding on to your grief may satisfy some need for self-punishment, it does nothing to free life for living.

When we recognize the loneliness and emptiness the death has caused for what it is, we relieve some of the distress it may bring about. We acknowledge that our life and our capacity to love have not ended. To deny the possibility of loving again because the object of our love is gone is to pass a death sentence on one's self. This process results in a hostile, resentful, sour personality that denies the right of love to exist. In fact, it encourages the opposite—hostility and hatred.

It is true that the pain of loneliness can be so great that a person feels as if something within him or her has died, too. However, the grieving person's task is to begin expressing love and caring in creative living. This can begin with the friends who gather to express condolence. By accepting their love and being willing to be the object of concern, a bereaved person adds something to his or her own life, and at the same time verifies an important process in the lives of others.

There is a difference between being alone and being lonely. Loneliness is an emotional state that may be quite painful, while being alone is a state of separation from others that can open doors to self-awareness and personal growth. During times of being alone, it is possible to:

- Do the reading that has been put off
- Listen to music that others dislike
- Learn to value our aloneness
- Grow comfortable with our self
- Develop resources that may be of great use to us
- Learn to value both times in our life—with our loved one and without

Great works of literature have come out of the experiences of persons who were alone. At the same time, we know that life becomes what it is through language, culture, and social relationships, and we would not dispense with them.

We all need to learn to value both times in our life: the time spent with others, and the time spent alone.

MARGE EATON HEEGAARD is the author of
Grieving and Growing Curriculum for Adult Grief Support Groups.
Used by permission from Woodland Press,
99 Woodland Circle, Minneapolis, MN 55424;
952-926-2556.

What Does Recovery Look Like?

Having more good days
Days seem brighter
Crying less and less
Physical health improves
Socializing again
Laughing feels okay
Memories bring pleasure without tears
Feeling like you once again "have a life"
Normal is a good word
Relationships improve
Being open to new relationships
Having hope for the future
Finding pleasure from worship services
Feeling that joy is returning

Broken Heart Syndrome

MARTY McNUNN

A few months ago a friend had a massive heart attack and died while driving on the freeway. His wife was able to get the car to the side of the road and call 911. She, too, was rushed to the hospital, believing she had also experienced a heart attack. However, she recovered quickly. The doctor diagnosed her condition as "broken heart syndrome." I had never heard this term. Here is what I have discovered (the following is excerpted from an article by Kathleen Fackelmann in *USA Today,* Health and Behavior section, February 9, 2005):

> A sudden shock, such as hearing news of a death in the family, can trigger a condition that appears to be a massive heart attack, except that the victim suffers no lasting heart damage, a study reports today.
>
> Researchers have dubbed this condition the "broken heart syndrome." It mimics a heart attack, leading doctors to believe the heart has suffered severe damage. But, instead, the heart is *temporarily* stunned. According to Johns Hopkins cardiologist Llan Wittstein, "Massive heart attacks don't get better within a matter of days."

Wittstein stumbled upon the syndrome after seeing a patient who had experienced what was described as a massive heart attack after learning of her mother's death. Within a short time, the Hopkins doctors were treating two more patients who had suffered an emotional shock and were displaying heart attack symptoms.

The team collected 19 cases for the study, persons whose symptoms suggested that a blockage (often a blood clot) interrupted blood flowing to the heart. "Tests found no sign of a blood clot or blockage, and no evidence to suggest that the heart tissue had been irreversibly damaged," says Wittstein. Two weeks later, patients' heart functions returned to normal, which is almost unheard of when someone has had a major heart attack.

Soon after the event occurred in these test cases, the doctors measured very high blood levels of catecholamine, which are stress hormones released after an emotional trauma. Subjects had catecholamine levels about 30 times higher than normal.

"The surge of stress hormones overwhelmed the heart, leaving the powerhouse unable to pump effectively," Wittstein says. After the shock subsided, the levels of stress hormones dropped, and the heart's pumping power returned.

In most cases of broken heart syndrome, people recover quickly, with no long-lasting medical problems.

How Adults Can Help Children Cope with Death and Grief

MARGE EATON HEEGAARD, MA, ATR, LICSW

In response to the death of a loved one, adults will seek additional support and education, both to understand their own grief process and to model a healthy reaction to loss by expressing their feelings and receiving support.

However, children will generally learn their response to a death from other adults in the family. Often, children may feel frightened and insecure because they sense the grief and stress of others, and feel powerless to help. They will need additional love, support, and structure in their daily routine at this time.

When someone dies, children often worry about themselves and other family members dying. They need to know who would take care of them in the unlikely death of both parents.

Children also need an adequate explanation of the cause of death, using correct terms like "die" and "dead." Using vague terms and trying to shield children from the truth merely adds confusion. Avoid terms that associate death with going away, sleep, or sickness. Listen carefully to a child's response.

Children have magical thinking and may believe that their behavior or thoughts can cause or reverse death.

Do not exclude children when family and friends come to

comfort grieving adults. Avoidance or silence teaches children that death is a taboo subject. Children need to learn how to cope with loss, not to be protected from grief.

Help children learn to recognize, name, accept, and express feelings; this helps them avoid developing unhealthy defenses for coping with difficult emotions. Make physical and creative activities available for energy outlets.

A child may try to protect grieving adults and attempt to assume the caretaking role, but children need to grow up normally without being burdened with adult responsibilities.

Help children learn to cope with other losses, too. For example, the death of a pet is a very significant loss for a child. The patterns for coping with loss and grief begin in early childhood and often continue thorough adulthood.

Share personal religious beliefs carefully. Children express feelings of grief more in behavior than in words. Feelings of abandonment, helplessness, despair, anxiety, apathy, anger, guilt, and fear are common, and these feelings are often acted out aggressively because children may be unable to express feelings verbally.

MARGE EATON HEEGAARD is the author of
Grieving and Growing Curriculum for Adult Grief Support Groups.
Used by permission from Woodland Press,
99 Woodland Circle, Minneapolis, MN 55424;
952-926-2556.

Comfort from the Bible

Grief

Psalm 23

Ecclesiastes 3:1–8

John 10:28

John 11:25–26

John 1:1–7

Revelations 21:4

1 Peter 1:21

2 Corinthians 5:9

Depression

Psalm 37:40

Isaiah 55:6

Jeremiah 29:11–13

Romans 8:28–31

John 14:27

Psalms 46:1–3

Isaiah 58:11

Joshua 1:9

2 Corinthians 12:9

Matthew 6:25–34

Healing

Psalm 41:4

Luke 4:18–19

James 5:13–16

Psalm 147:3

1 Peter 2:24

Isaiah 53:5

Thanksgiving

Psalm 50:14–15	Psalm 103:1–5
Psalm 100	Revelation 7:11–12
Psalm 107:1–3	James 1:1–4
Psalm 106:1–2	Psalm 118:1–4

Assurance of Salvation

Acts 16:31	Luke 5:32
John 3:16–18	John 20:31
John 3:3	1 John 1:9
Romans 10:17	Hebrews 11:6

Hastings Area
Grief Coalition

Hastings Area Grief Coalition

———

MARTY McNUNN, Minister of Congregational Care
United Methodist Church of Hastings, Minnesota

Retired nurse Jan Junkman and I often discussed the need for additional support for bereaved families in our community. As a result, Jan volunteered to serve as "Bereavement Pastor" at the Methodist Church. Her task would be to work with a family who had lost a loved one, especially assisting with preparations for the funeral service and the lunch following.

About that same time, a local Sunday newspaper ran an article about a grief group that was meeting in St. Paul—one of thirteen such groups in the Metro Area Grief Coalition.

Jan and I talked to Lois Knutson, lead facilitator for the St. Paul group, and were invited to visit her group meeting. It seemed to be just what we were looking for in the Hastings area. Lois volunteered to be our mentor us as we formed our own group.

We decided to offer an informational meeting about a proposed grief coalition in Hastings, and sent invitations to pastors in the Hastings area. About twenty people accepted. At this meeting, Lois shared her experience of losing her daughter, and her involvement in grief groups following that death.

From that initial meeting, six or eight people expressed interest in pursuing a group for Hastings. Over the next six months, this group met regularly to lay the groundwork for a Grief Coalition in the Hastings area.

We chose to follow the program of the Area Grief Coalition; it was working well for the other groups, and we had no other plan to follow. We used the manual and workbook that Marge Heegaard, founder of Grief Coalitions, had published to assist new groups.

Ms. Heegaard's format consisted of thirty minutes for listening to an educational speaker, and then breaking into small groups with people who had suffered similar losses. Each group, whether dealing with spouse loss, child loss, parent loss, etc., had a facilitator who had also experienced the same loss. The weekly topics of education were based on a thirteen-week rotation, so every thirteen weeks we began a new education series and changed locations, giving all participating churches a chance to host the group.

Our first official meeting was held on November 2, 2000, and a large group attended. About a year later, the local senior center offered its facilities as a permanent home. Since then we have met every Thursday evening from 6:00 until 7:30, using the original format.

My plan was to organize the group, then to give the responsibility of the weekly meeting to someone else. But God had other plans.

I tearfully confessed to a dear friend that I did not want to be involved. "God will not make you do something do not want to do," he said. "If this is His plan, He will place a joy in your heart for doing this work, and you will not be able to resist being involved."

And it's true: just as my friend had predicted, God has placed a joy in my heart that wells up when I am dealing with the grief ministry. Yes, God had a plan for Hastings, and I am a part of it, currently serving as the Lead Facilitator for the weekly grief coalition meetings. We are working out His plan and seeing grieving people come to life again after learning to live with their grief, and this is immensely fulfilling for me.

It takes courage to attend a grief group meeting for the first time.
It is a fearful thing to expose your sorrow.
Once you master the courage and go, you will find others
hurting just as you do, who will listen to your story, share their story,
and with common thoughts and feelings begin
to walk through your grief together.

Grief Support Groups

———

LYLA DAVIES

My husband died in 1991 after a long and painful battle with cancer. At that time there were no grief support groups in the Hastings area, so a pastor from my church agreed to host one. When participants from several churches responded positively to the proposed group, we recognized a need in our community.

Later, I took a facilitator training course and several seminars on grief support, gaining an education on grief issues and learning to facilitate small groups.

A few years later, the original support group had evolved into a six-week Grief Education and Support Course, offered twice a year, spring and fall. Some of the topics covered are:

1. Overview of grief
2. Emotional aspects of grief
3. Grief and the family
4. Spiritual aspects of grief
5. Self-care in grief
6. Taking the next step

Facilitators are trained to lead the group discussion. Even though individuals participating in the mixed group have different losses, the grieving process is central to everyone's loss.

———

At the conclusion of the six weeks, the participants are encouraged to continue on their journey through grief, perhaps joining an ongoing support group.

At this time, I am also involved in the Hastings Area Grief Coalition, which meets once a week. This group was formed to satisfy the evident need for an ongoing source of support.

Educational speakers at our meetings cover subjects such as:

- Feelings and emotions
- Journey through grief
- Roadblocks of grief
- Grief and family
- Grief and faith
- Recurring grief
- What do I do now?
- Taking care of yourself
- Remembering when
- What's normal?
- Does it ever end?
- Telling a personal story

People come as long as they need to: some leave and come back again and again as they feel the need.

In the Grief Coalition Group, as in the Education and Support Group, a "Service of Remembering" is held twice a year. Group participants bring a picture to share and a story to tell, and then light a candle in memory of their loved one.

General rules for both an Education and Support Course and a Grief Coalition Support Group are as follows:

1. Begin and end on time
2. Welcome participants
3. Use name tags
4. Stress confidentiality

5. Listen but do not judge

6. Do not offer advice

7. Provide breaks and refreshments

8. Ensure equal time for all participants

9. Accept that situations can't be changed or fixed

10. Have tissues available!

11. Offer hugs at the end of each session

These two groups complement and reinforce each other. Grieving is a process unique to each individual, so providing a variety of supports is the best method of helping individuals in their grief journey.

Two are better than one:
Because they have a good return in their work;
If one falls down, his friend will help him up.
But pity the one who falls and has no one to help him up!

—Ecclesiastes 4:9–10 (NIV)

Comments of an Innocent Bystander

DAVID BAUDOIN
Hastings Cable Access Television

It's my role to tape the grief group speakers for broadcast over our local cable access television station. For that reason, I see the process differently from the way the grieving person who attends a weekly gathering sees it.

When I first started preparing these tapes, I was a rather detached person just doing his job. But, as time went on, I found myself being pulled in more and more by the force that seems to be present in that group setting.

Time after time, I saw grieving people return and gain additional strength to make it through another week. I observed them shyly looking from side to side, discovering they weren't alone on an "Island of Grief."

Some participants improved rapidly and some at a snail's pace, but, without exception, they all improved.

Through it all, I gained a deeper understanding of the grief process, more compassion for people involved in the process, and a better acceptance of death as a part of life.

I've been fortunate in my years to have been grief-free, but I know that if I were to suddenly lose my wife, a child, or my mom, I'd head straight for a grief group family, and turn the camera work over to someone else.

Acknowledgments

I awoke very early one morning thinking I'd had a dream. My mind was so full of images to sort through that I got up and wrote down what I was thinking for fear I'd forget by morning. I came to realize that what I was seeing on that paper was the idea for a book that needed to be written. So I must thank the Lord for the inspiration. I believe this book has a purpose and that it will help many hurting people.

Many thanks to those who have participated in the Hastings grief group over the years. I know it took courage to come that first time. I have learned so much from you because of your pain. Even though you may not have contributed your story for this book, you will find yourself on its pages, see where you were, and see how much you have recovered since that first meeting.

I am grateful for friends and family who were willing to edit and rewrite. Thanks to Jim Biegel, Pat Walker, Lisa Graham, Donna Mathiowetz, Sallee Jepsen, David and Elaine Baudoin, Pastor Jeff Utecht, and Marge Heegaard for reading, making suggestions, and correcting.

Lew Linde, thanks for reading the manuscript and for your

suggestions, your legal explanations, and for recommending Prism Publishing.

Chris Garrick, you are an inspiration. Thanks for believing in me and the need for this book; also, for listening to my rambling thoughts in the early months. I enjoyed our lunches. Thanks for your encouragement and for your editing skills and suggestions for improvement.

Bev Finke, words escape me to be able to express my thanks for the hours and hours you volunteered to editing, rewriting, formatting, and encouraging me all the way. You have been an incredible help.

Karrie Hamilton: thanks for listening and believing in what once seemed impossible. Our long walks and conversations helped keep me on the right track.

Mary Tessness, thanks for driving "Ms. Marty" to and from the publisher's appointments. You are more than a coworker; you are a true friend.

Jerry Matula, you are my computer man. I am thankful I have a friend like you to come to my rescue when the computer didn't do what I wanted it to do. Thanks for your time.

Pastor Michael Graham and the Hastings United Methodist Church Prayer Team and my coworkers who have faithfully prayed for those working on the manuscript: thanks for caring.

To my Syren Books team, Maria Manske, Wendy Holdman, Kyle Hunter, and Mary Byers. Thank you for making a dream come true. You are a great team.

Last, but certainly not least, to my wonderful family, I want to express my thanks for believing in me, and for listening when I just needed to talk about "the book." Thanks also for encouraging me, and for your prayers and financial commitment that made this book a reality.

My family includes my daughters, Nanci Ladd and Vivian

Walker; their respective spouses, Jon and Patrick; my son, John McNunn; grandchildren Jessica and Mike Mraz, Kara and Cess Mercado, Andrea Howard, Nyki and Jim Biegel, Austin and Tyler Walker, and Justin Howard, as well as the little ones, McKenna, Jordan, and Abigayle.

You are the best. I am blessed because of you.

About the Author

MARTY McNUNN currently serves as Minister of Congregational Care for the United Methodist Church in Hastings, Minnesota. In 2000 she coordinated the formation of a weekly grief group in her community and continues as the Lead Facilitator.

She is a Certified Grief ❣ Recovery Specialist® with The Grief Recovery Institute® in Sherman Oaks, California.

Prior to moving to Hastings, Marty served as a missionary with Youth With a Mission (YWAM), where she received a Biblical Counselors Certificate from the College of Counseling and Health Care in Kona, Hawaii.

Marty's children, grandchildren, and great-grandchildren live in Minnesota and California.